BUILT FOR IT!

BUILT FOR IT!

KRYSTAL A. HUGHES

Krystal A. Hughes

Contents

Preface

Singing, "Here we go again nnnnnnnnnnnnnnnnnnn!" This sound/ phrase from the TikTok video really sums up my feelings as I begin to write again. Here I go again, writing another book, I'm sure many people can relate to, even though it chronicles more trauma, heartbreak, and healing in my life. I know what you're thinking, you'll be like, "What has happened now?" Especially those of you who read the first book (Read My Story, Hear God's Glory). Like you, I also thought that my healing journey was on the more positive end and that I had made it through the worst of things and I could now breathe/soar. I was so ready to debut my 1st book and then do book tours, speaking engagements, and whatever else God had in store for me. In my mind, I had it all figured out and I was in a very good space. I had spent the summer writing, reading the New Testament of the Bible, healing on a new level, and doing weekly and sometimes daily prayer calls with my family and friends. I had also been in my new place in Atlanta for a bit, hitting every social event, hanging out with my friends, and spending time with my family. My father and I had completed therapy and were now back on speaking terms. I was in a good space, emotionally, physically, and mentally. I was dreaming again, making plans, good tangible plans that I figured were beyond me just making money or being popular, but working and walking in my purpose. I know that one of my callings is to be a healer and through my writings and touring, I was going to be able to do just that, help others heal. At the very least, hopefully, people would read it and know that there is someone out there who truly understands every emotion they are feeling. It's nothing like feeling understood and I would feel very accomplished if I was able to be that understanding person for those who had no one else. What I can say is from the feedback of readers I did just that. On September 25, 2022, I did a light release of my first book. Since releasing my book with no push, no branding, and no advertisement other than me post-ing on my socials of maybe a combined 5,000 people, my book which God graced me to write has touched everyone who has completed it. The reviews speak for themselves on Amazon. People always inbox me on socials and tell me how they are touched by my book or tell me their own stories with experiences like mine. I am so grateful that somebody somewhere read it and was able to get something from it. That is why I am back again, willing to share all the testing and lessons I have endured and learned in this season. I am depending on God every day in every way and awaiting the shift in my life and, in the meantime, keeping my Faith strong. I've faced new challenges and have had new experiences (some rooted in old situations). Just like the last book, this book is also a tool to be used for healing, motivation, insight, inspiration, and/or education. We are not all facing the same things at the same time, but who knows, one day you may face the very same thing or similar things. One major thing I write about in this book that I know we all will face is grief. Here's my current story!

2

Introduction

October 28, 2022, I am back home in Birmingham, Alabama for my grandmother's 75th birthday! I can't wait to celebrate with her the next day! I had been making plans since the month started. I tried to get her to do a photo shoot and everything, but she would not do it, lol. So we settled on going to Fleming's for dinner. I had invited everyone and we were going to all have a ball. The day before, October 28th, she and I went shopping and she picked out some dresses, her face just lit up in the mirror when I begged her to try on the ones she thought wouldn't flatter her, and to her surprise, they did! We had so much fun that day, and after shopping she left ready for her birthday dinner. I promised to get up early and come over and do her makeup and everything before we went out.

Fast forward, to the 29th, I am outside hanging with my homegirl, Kameisha. We were gearing up to enjoy one of the biggest weekends in the city, Magic City Classic weekend. It's the weekend in which two rival HBCUs, Alabama A & M and Alabama State go head to head on the field in football, band competition, and tailgates, for bragging rights until the next year. It's a festive time with events spanning an entire week and always lands near my grandmother's birthday. So, I wasn't going to miss it while in town. Plus, I hadn't participated in years due to living overseas and then the pandemic, so this was about to be a time. It was just that, "A Time," we got dressed up and headed straight to the stadium. We ended up bumping into everyone we knew. I spent time with old friends and co-workers and ran into people I hadn't seen in years. It was a beautiful day with perfect weather, I looked good, felt good, and was having a blast. The day was going good and honestly couldn't be any better. As night fell, we decided to attend the adult skate night event. On our way to the skating rink, my middle sister called and told me to let her know when I was leaving the rink so we could get together for the rest of the night. I told her, "Cool, I would." She called me again when I got to the skating rink and told me the same thing and I told her again, okay. I put on my skates, go around the rink maybe one time, and here my sister is calling me again. I ignored her because obviously, this must be a mistake. We just talked two times in less than an hour. I go around again and they play my song and she calls again, although annoyed at this point, I answer and nothing could prepare me for what she was about to say on the phone. Nothing throughout that day or even this time would have signified that she would be calling me to tell me that our youngest sister had been murdered. My baby sister, a 30-year-old, widowed, single mother of two was dead. As she spoke the words, I couldn't believe them. I skated off the rink without even realizing how or when I did. I kicked my skates off and went outside with nothing but socks on to make sure I heard her correctly. As I began to ask questions to clarify, she told me to hold on, she then clicked back over with the manager at the hotel where my sister was murdered and the manager then told us verbatim what had happened. My baby sister was dead and I told my other sister I was on the way and hung up. I whispered in Kameisha's ear what happened and went to the car, I don't know how she got her shoes back on so quickly, that by the time I found the keys to the car, she and our other friend were at the car telling me I could not drive.

I just obliged and let Kameisha drive. We cried and prayed, and they held me the whole way to the hotel.

As I got out of the car and walked up, I was met by the detective. She quickly told me her name, verified my name and gave her condolences. She then told me my sister's body was no longer there and that she needed an answer on where her body should go. She had been asking my mother and sister over and over and neither of them was coherent enough to even give a name. I never in my life had to do this before. I'm 33 years old, and anybody that has ever died in my family, the elders handled it. At this point, the only elder left in my immediate family is my grandmother and she was home with the kids trying to calm them, especially my nephew, my sister's oldest son. So, here I am thinking of funeral homes and finally was able to come up with one. After that, something just clicked and I told my friends that I was going to have to get things done because I could already see and sense there was no one that was going to be stable enough to handle it. After that, we were allowed up to my sister's room to collect her things, all of her things. She was about to move into a new place, so in the meantime, she had been living in this room with her two kids. Things were everywhere, we had to get everything, all the baby clothes, shoes, the big boy things, her things, all her intimate items, panties, bras, shoes, clothes, every-thing. All I could think was "Why was she staying in this room?" This was literally a motel-level place in one of the roughest parts of town. We weren't on speaking terms, but there is no way if she had asked me that I would have let her, let alone my 12-year-old nephew or 1-year-old niece stay here. As I packed, I was just in disbelief, anger, and incredible sadness. My sister is gone y'all and, to put the icing on the cake, my estranged mother and other sister told me she kept calling me because my youngest sister wanted to surprise me. Her goal was to see and talk to me before the end of the night.

3

Kernisha Jenay Hughes (McClinon)

My sister, Ms. Kernisha Jenay Hughes (McClinon at death), was born to our parents, the same mother and father. She was the youngest of the three of us girls, the baby. Very soft spoken, beautiful, goofy, with the longest, prettiest lashes you could ever see. She had beautiful full thick hair that grew everywhere on her, all down her temples. She had beautiful eyes, a light brown hue at times, she had a beautiful small gap that when she let go and wasn't ashamed of her gap, she smiled big, and her smile shined brightly. She was a little taller than the rest of us 5'4" shorties, standing somewhere between 5'5" and 5'7". She had a naturally beautiful shape and a light brown olive-shade complexion. She was beautiful, she struggled to see it, but she was definitely a beauty. She died so young, I can't really tell you how great she may have been at her fullest potential. She was a lot of things, but one thing I have to give her is that she did well with my nephew. She raised him to be mannerable, meek, and loving. The things she taught him just oozes out of him. He is only 13 years old, tall, broad, and looks like a giant. He is so gentle, caring, and listens well, nothing like most kids his age. I can only attribute that to her, because, since the time he was born he has been in her care and her care alone. Then there is my niece who is 2 years old and smart as a whip and looks exactly like my sister. It's hard looking at her sometimes because she resembles her so much. She even has the same attitude and personality. My sister was really sweet when she warmed up and got to know people, but in the beginning, she was not very welcoming and my niece is the exact same way. That was my sister though, I spent so much of our younger years babying that girl! Nobody could bother her, not even my mother and nobody could come in between us, not even my other sister. We were thick as thieves. When I finally got my own room, I would go get her out of her bed in the middle of the night and put her in the bed with me. I always took care of my sisters when my mother wasn't around and even a lot of times when she was.

I was a mother figure to them for a long time, until we went to DHR and were split up. I won't divulge all of the DHR matters again here (go read the first book, it's all there), but I will give our history and why we were estranged in the most honorable way possible. In the midst of being in DHR at 17 years old, I was declared a dependent of the state/an adult, those who read the previous book know that by now. So, I was living on my own with my then-boyfriend. Soon after him and I moved in together, my sister asked to come live with me. The state did a background check and check of my home and determined that she could stay with us. We all, me and my sisters, by that time had all changed either for better or for worse. Being split up like we were and living outside of our parents' care, a lot of new demons had time to arise in our lives. My sister was like 11 or 12 when we got taken out of the home. So, it hit her much harder and a lot differently than the rest of us. She had not even begun to fully understand what was happening and we did not have much support mentally or emotionally to help us understand or alleviate the anguish we were experiencing. Me and my other sister could comprehend a lot more than she could. She also was a lot more impressionable than us.

While living in the care of our foster mom, my sisters were exposed to a totally different lifestyle than me when I stopped living there. They were introduced to sex and a lot of other things that kids their age should not be exposed to. My sister was like 13 with an 18-year-old boyfriend. Also, later had to take the stand as a witness against our then-foster brother/play cousin in a murder case. So, she was growing up very fast and starting to exhibit behavioral issues. She came to live with me and my boyfriend. She would act out at school and I would have to catch two buses across town to get to her school and plead with her administrators to not put her out or talk some sense in to her. She would leave with her boyfriend without telling me or just do anything that was reckless or against what we were asking her to do. I know she had been through a lot, we all had, but I needed her to just do right while I was in school. My school eventually threatened to put me out if I left school again. At that point, I had to give her up, it was either that or fail out of high school myself. I tried, my boyfriend tried, we tried everything we could for her to get on track and stay on track but there was nothing else we could do. Unbeknownst to me until now, that was the first real break in our relationship.

After her moving out and as we started to grow older, we all (me, my sisters, and our mother) just began living in a chaotic, toxic, interdependent relationship. I was in college, while both of my sisters were running around in the streets, just like my mother did. She was constantly enabling them, trying to make up for her previous failures. I would mainly hear from them when someone was in trouble or they needed something. I was still mothering even at this point of me being 20, my other sister 19 and pregnant, and my youngest 17 and pregnant. My sister was so young and had so much on her shoulders. She now had this baby and was not prepared to be a mother. She was 17 and the father had run off before she conceived. So now she's 17, a single mom, going through postpartum, poor, filled with childhood trauma, and trying to make it the best she knew how. She took a lot of roads, not always the best, but she took roads so she and her son could live well and cope with all we had been through. We often argued because I tried to give her direction. I started traveling doing contracts for work and that pissed her off. She told me she felt like I was abandoning her, but I was not her parent and had to do what was needed for me, for all of us really, because now I'm helping out with the kids financially as well. Then she had a mental break. I did not do any assignments for a while and tried to be there for her and care for her. She lashed out at me and anyone else around her who tried to tell her the correct ways to do things. It's hard to do and see what's right when you're being taught and influenced by what's wrong. She literally became a product of the environment we lived in, although she kept it together on the outside amongst strangers, she still silently suffered. She was tormented and she tormented those around her. I had to break away from her and our whole toxic 4-some (me, her, my other sister, and our mother). I tried getting us all counseling before I left to go overseas to work, but we only completed one session. The therapist was not equipped to take on the multiple issues we had and I was the only one truly willing to work on our relationships. I left and nothing ever got resolved.

***

Fast forward to 2019 when my other sister was charged with murdering her baby's father, my youngest sister and I had this huge blowup. Regardless of what went on, we always protected each other. My youngest sister really was not operating in the way we normally would and everyone around us that had any knowledge of what had happened was calling me. Everyone was telling me what my youngest was saying and doing. The things she was saying could have been detrimental to my other sister's case. I had no choice but to talk to her and that conversation and text did not go well. I had at this time been holding my peace with her on several occasions. She had shown her tail to me in front of my aunt's condo. She had shown her tail at my then-youngest niece's baby shower and so many other things. So, at this point, I had to let her know what it was and how I felt and we no longer talked until I came home in 2021. She called me and we talked briefly. She was pregnant again now with my niece and we talked about various things, what she would name the baby, her thoughts about having the baby, our relationship, and where we stood. The conversation ended abruptly, but before we ended, I asked her what issue she had with me and told her that if she could tell me I would apologize. The only thing she came up with is that she didn't like the way I said things sometimes, again the conversation ended abruptly and nothing came from that. I didn't hear from her again until the beginning of 2022. It was not a good encounter. Then I saw her in the summer when I was picking the kids up, she spoke, I spoke, we exchanged the kids and went about our business. She looked good again, I mentioned it to Kameisha who had rode with me to get the kids. She looked healthy, she laughed at me cracking on my sister's raggedy truck and that was the last time I would see her alive. A very short life, riddled with trauma, pain, and hurt. I wished she lived longer to get fully healed, to be here for her kids, and ideally live a greater later life than her former life. I loved her dearly and have no regrets about us being estranged. I tried and tried and tried and tried and tried and tried and tried with my sister. I do wish we had that last conversation she wanted to have at Classic. I also don't think she deserved to be murdered so cruelly, but like the old saying goes, you never know the place, time, or how you're going to leave this Earth. I shifted my focus from how she died, with the understanding that somehow, someway, we all have to go. So, I leave it alone with the simple thought that God has His plans and I'm grateful to know she made it in.

4

Taking it all in

Here I am still trying to wrap my head around my sister being murdered. Crying on and off and talking to what feels like a thousand people. At some point, my father, three of my aunties, and I got on the phone. Everyone is just talking and Kameisha is just running back and forth from room to room asking if I need anything, trying to feed me, briefly stopping to dry my tears, making my bed for me, etc. and then my eldest aunt on the phone began to prophesy to me. She told me that I had to be strong because I was going to have to plan and do everything concerning the funerals (which I had already grasped from that short amount of time in the hotel room). She told me that things would get really ugly and hard, that God was going to cover me every step of the way, that I just had to keep moving forward, and that if I completed this mission a blessing would be waiting for me. I heard her, but I was in such a trance of hurt that I didn't think much of it. I was too busy still trying to understand things I had answers to but still did not comprehend at the moment. Like, why was my sister in this motel? Why didn't she call me? Why would this man kill her? What would happen to the kids? How do I plan a funeral? Is this real? It felt so fake and so surreal that I thought I was having a vivid bad dream.

I woke up on Oct. 30th, 2022, my grandmother's 75th birthday, and everything that had happened really happened. This was real and now we did have more info on what and why. A deranged man who was living at the same motel as her asked her for her number and when she didn't oblige, he shot her about 5 times. The fatal shot was the one to the chest that punctured and ruptured her aorta. Not only did he kill her, he also carjacked a family at gunpoint and then proceeded to run from the police. He led them on a high-speed chase which eventually ended with him plowing through a 60-year-old man riding his bike. Many families were traumatized that night and many families were hurt. The hurt didn't stop there, we made the bad decision of going to see my sister's body straight out of the autopsy, I would not recommend this to anyone, but we wanted to see her so bad and through a family connection, we were allowed. There she lay, my baby sister's body all cut up from the autopsy, eyes closed and lifeless, a bullet through her cheek and cold, so cold. The one thing that stood out to me was that she was so cold. I was screaming so loud with a voice I didn't even recognize as my own and louder than anyone in the room. This was torture and I only wanted them to cover her up, because she was cold. The other thing I remember is how beautiful even in this state, I thought she was. I know that's a crazy thing to think of but I remember settling down and crying silently and telling Kameisha who was right there by my side how long her lashes were, how her hair was beautifully cascading down her forehead and face. She was my baby sister and even through the hardships, strife, and trauma we endured, I still loved her and saw her as the little baby I used to defend, hold, and take her out of her own bed to sleep with me. They took us out, we were all hollering and my nephew was uncontrollable. We had seen enough and now I just wanted to make her burial right. We couldn't start on anything, because this was the weekend. A Sunday and nothing could be done until Monday. So, we went back to my sister's house and did what the family did when someone died. Everyone visited, even estranged family members and we ate and spoke of the memories that we had of my sister. We did that all day and night until people started to go home.

Monday came and we got to the funeral home to make arrangements. It's still such a bizarre thing. Me, my mother, and other sister began to pick out everything, how many family cars, what church, what colors, newspaper write-up or not, police escort, her casket (which we let my nephew pick out), and just everything significant and controlled by the funeral home. You go over every detail and Ms. Carolyn at Robert's funeral home in Birmingham, AL on Bessemer superhighway was such a pleasant woman. She took her time with us, she was so compassionate and very empathetic and walked us through everything step by step. Without her, we would never have been able to get through the process as well as we did. People mostly go to funerals, but most don't plan them. My mom, sister, and I started off planning everything together and then the rest fell on me. I and one of my aunts paid for her funeral, I made and typed out her obituary (which was very hard, again we were estranged), and made sure that everyone had the proper clothing for the funerals (The kids, my mother, and her boyfriend, my sister and her husband), permed and did my mother's hair (whom I hadn't talked to in two years at this point). My grandmother's brother, my great uncle, paid for the repast and his in-laws cooked and served at the repast along with other family members and a few of my old coworkers and close friends. I did a lot of things that I had never in my life done before or knew how to do, but God graced me. Things really came together and I only have one regret throughout any of it and I know God is going to turn that around as well. My sister's funeral proceeded and went extremely well and after it was time for me to go back home.

***

Not only was my youngest sister murdered, but 2 weeks later my grandmother died, and 5 months later my other sister was found guilty of murdering her ex-boyfriend. Both of my sisters left behind 2 kids of their own, 3 girls, and 1 boy. From the time of death all the way up even until now, March 8, 2024, it has been a whirlwind. I feel like I am no longer able to be the carefree single woman traveling the world I used to be because now I am making decisions that not only benefit me but also my nieces and nephews, assisting with raising them and trying to be there for my mother. Whether I wanted to or not, I was definitely chosen to and built for it. By God, my family, and everyone else in between. I did not ask to be in this position, nor did I volunteer, things just flowed to me. Unfortunately, for me, even though this was what I was destined to do at that time, it came with great resentment and a lot of jealousy. I was secretly hated for being the responsible and trusted one that everyone came to. People would come straight to me with questions, inquiries, etc. People would say to me, you have to get the kids, you can't let them be raised the way you guys were. I was under a great deal of pressure literally at all times. Also, everything surrounding my sister was in the media, because her death was broadcasted all over the news and social media. There was no hiding from it, I could not even grieve in peace, because I also needed to make sure to clean up all the false narratives that were put out. Many people were questioning why my sister was staying in a room and to further assassinate her charter some were alluding to her being involved in some type of illegal activity while there and trying to falsely say this was why she was murdered. Then it was the random people reaching out to me and other family members with, "information." Only one of all those people was legit and when it came down to her telling what she knew, she backed out (more on this later). Then some people said the accused had been released on bail, again another false narrative that we had to debunk, beyond just saying that wasn't true, there was a lot of emotional turmoil surrounding it. My mother was literally a zombie and her mind was very manic. She would call me, and sometimes still do, in an emotional uproar about what others had said. She was all over the place and was also very terrified because people were making the murderer and his family out to be these invincible people who somehow were capable of going beyond what he had already done and attacking our family. It was a constant rollercoaster and I had only one choice, which was to take everything on the chin, be the leader, and represent the family.

There were a few primary people (Kameisha, Tomica, Nicole, Shenita, Nikki, Naamonde, Cheyenne and my therapist) who really helped me maintain my own sanity throughout that time. I'm grateful for those people, but there were still a lot of uncalled-for things going on. I had one aunt try to talk to me about my first book, honestly, that was not the time, nor the place. A different aunt tried to critique me on handling some things with the funeral, not asking to help or gently guide me on it, but rather criticizing and fussing. This was not the right time for any of that, very small things, but more things added on top of everything else I was already experiencing. I did not say much during this time and did not even react to things. I prayed a lot, journaled, and spoke with my therapist. She would stop in the middle of a session and pray for me. Then she would turn around and prophecy to me. God was sending me people in the midst, but all I really wanted to do was retreat and get to myself back in Georgia. This is how I am, I am a processor and like to sort things out on my own. I could not do that while constantly being amongst others. I was so happy when I was able to return home that Sunday night. I went by to visit my family, kissed my grandmother on the cheek, and set out to Atlanta. On my way to Atlanta, I kind of got my mind together. I decided that I was going to take this grief thing seriously and dive into therapy, work, and work-out. I had really pulled myself together and was ready for my first-day orientation at my brand-new job. I realized God was stretching me in this season and that I could get through it, but I wasn't prepared for how far and how much he was going to stretch me. As I was walking into my job orientation, signing my name, and getting a badge, I got the call that my grandmother had passed.

5

Freada Joyce Hughes

Freada Joyce Hughes was born on October 30, 1947, the woman I would grow to love and call Grandma. My granny, well really my mother, because just about everything I am, I've learned, and how I behave stems from her. She was the greatest in my eyesight, of course with faults, because no human is perfect. I literally lived in her shadows for the majority of my childhood, I'm grateful for that, there is no way I would be all that I am without her guidance and raising. Strong as an Ox, mean as a whip some would say about her, after all, she was a baby boomer and those people were/are hard workers. In addition to that I would call her a strong woman of God. To this day, I find little notes and highlights in her Bible where she was spending time in her word; I would also call her a warrior. She defended her family fiercely even to some faults as you guys read in my previous book. She was loving, she would go out of her way and do anything for anybody, especially her family. I mean anything, cook, clean for them, nurse them back to health, let them borrow money, let people stay with us, she would give her last, go out on a limb for people and again, especially for her family. She was a woman of service, it came naturally and she enjoyed doing it. She was beautiful, with high yellow, almost white skin (she hated for anyone to say that, lol), and beautiful long black hair that gray only slightly penetrated during her aging. A beautiful smile, when she did smile, because she rarely did. She was a very stern woman, who believed in decency and order and was not the one to be played with. She stood 5'4 like the rest of us, but the heart of a lion. She could beat a face, even though she had naturally beautiful skin and thick eyebrows and nails that grew longer and stronger than most people's nail extensions. She loved to look nice! She was so big on us looking presentable and I really had to think back and just realized she always looked well wherever she went and wanted the same for us. She was smart, always reading, doing crossword puzzles, counting, and working.

As for me, I was her pride and joy. Some people say favorite, but honestly, she loved all of us the same. I think we just happened to connect better and have more in common. There is nothing that she did for me that she wouldn't have done for my sisters. I just so happened to be the oldest, her first grandbaby, and the one who listened the most. She was always teaching. She taught me how to cook, clean, crotchet, sew, take care of everything, and use my common sense. She taught me about God, she always took us to church, dragging, kicking, and screaming. She wanted us to know God. She taught me work ethic, I watched her always go to work and never miss a day even when she was sick. She was a provider for us, her mother, and our mother for many years, and sometimes other family members as well. Again she was my everything and on the way home from my sister's funeral in that limo, she told us she was tired and that she would not be here long. She meant it, exactly four days after my sister's funeral, I got the call that she had passed. She passed in her sleep, and although this is something that still saddens me, I'm grateful for it. She always told me she did not want to die like my great-grandmother on a ventilator and wanted to just pass in her sleep. I'm thankful God granted her that wish of passing peacefully. As much as it hurts and I hate living on this earth without her, I'm also at peace. My grandmother lived to be 75 years old. She had seen so much and lost so many people, her son, her mother, her great-grandparents, a brother, my sister, and so many other people. I think she had nothing left in her, I remember at my sister's funeral, she was trying to get off the pew to get up and help contain my nephew that not even four grown men that were greater in size and number could contain. She couldn't stand up by herself due to one of her arms being stiff and not fully usable. This was because of a previous stroke and everyone was screaming at her, telling her there was no way she could help him. I think that 'not being able to help him' broke her and I feel like she felt that she had no more use on this earth. Even though to me, that could be farther from the truth.

She lived through the civil rights movement and watched black people go from poor servants to seeing Obama win the Presidency (something she often squealed about). She had raised her brothers, sisters, her kids, her nieces and nephews, and her grandkids and even was helping raise her great-grandkids. She went to college, earned a degree, and worked in hospitals for over 30 years. She was twice a retiree. And most importantly to me, she was my grandmother, the person who saw me, even in my worst, she saw my greatest and wanted me to aim for the stars in everything I did. After we had our shaky moments in our relationship (discussed in the previous book) she one day said to me, you remind me of my grandmother and I get you now. From then on, we rarely had any shaky moments and, if we did, it was caused by other people. We grew to become best friends. When I got older, I started to take care of her the same way she took care of me. If it was up to her she would be my shadow the same way I was hers as a kid. I did all I could when I could, but with working and living overseas, her being my shadow was not feasible. I am glad for the time we spent. When I moved back home in December 2020, I was with her if not every week, but several times a week. We did everything together, went shopping, went out to eat, to the nail shop, hair shop, movies, you name it, we did it. Again, she was my best friend and I knew I was hers. She leaves an undeniable legacy, one that I can only hope to live up to in my own way. People often speak about the things she did for them and what she meant to them. I know she meant a great deal to them, but to me, she was my everything.

6

⧜

Funeral #2 (One of the worst funerals in history)

Nothing could have prepared me for that call, my grandmother, my mother, my world? Nothing, but somehow I was calm enough to leave work, go back home repack, and drive right back to Birmingham. As I drove, family members called and talked to me the entire drive. My father's sister talked to me privately and said to me, I know how close you and your grandmother were, but please let your Mom and uncle do her arrangements. Also, she wanted me to rest because I had just done everything for my sister's funeral. I understood the hierarchy and promised not to overstep boundaries. As soon as I stepped out of the car, I was bombarded, by family, friends, and their sympathy. My grandmother's body was already gone and we were all just sitting around taking it all in. I was so shell-shocked and in disbelief. Also, I wasn't very comfortable around most of these people, so I didn't cry much ever at my sister's house. My grandmother had been staying at my sister's house for the past 3 months so we were gathered there. It was a mix of estranged family members and my sister's friends whom I was not a fan of.

Later, my uncle returned and he and my mother came to me and asked me to plan my grandmother's funeral because of how good I did my sister's funeral and how good she looked in the casket. Also, me and my uncle were the only two listed on her policy. I said okay and that was that. I was back in active mode and whatever grieving I thought I could do was again put on the back burner and I had to lead and stand up for my family. I mean, I had just done it, I should have been able to do this with my eyes closed, right? Wrong, my grandmother's funeral was a stark contrast to my sister's and did not honor my grandmother's legacy at all. She was a woman of decency and order and took a lot of pride in her family being viewed well. I mean, the planning part was pretty straight forward and Ms. Carolyn at Robert's funeral home really treated us like family. She even came to the house when she first got wind of my grandmother's death. Everyone was shaken by the events and just like there were beautiful, loving spirits surrounding us, there were dark ugly ones as well; the devil was about to use everyone he could. My grandmother was very light-skinned, so I know her body could not stay out long or risk turning colors, etcetera . She died on Monday and I had her funeral set for Friday. I had no idea this was or was going to be a problem, but take note here. Then my great uncle who took over the repass for my sister, he and his family decided to take over the repass again. So, things were being set pretty smoothly, thus far, but then the villains came out to play. This is where some of the exposure of people's true feelings and character started to show.

Before diving in, remember, during my sister's funeral my father's sister prophesied to me and told me that there was going to be great turmoil and confusion during the funeral and that God wanted me to remain strong and close to Him during this time. My sister's funeral was so smooth, that I was like, hmm, maybe she was wrong about that part of the prophecy. Well, neither God nor her mentioned my grandmother was going to die and everything she prophesied to me during my sister's funeral would come to fruition during my grandmother's. The first thing that happened was an energy shift. It was like the closeness me and my other living sister had had dissolved out of nowhere. It became really weird. I mean even at the funeral home when we were making plans for my grandmother's funeral and I said to her upon entering the room give me a hug, and she did, but as she was hugging me, she said to me I'm trying not to lash out at you. I honestly just did not even pay it any mind, because she had been showing out, being mean, and nasty to almost everyone, and having outbursts since my sister's funeral. My grandmother, mother, and I had talked to her and told her she was being very abrasive and needed to maybe get back on her meds or something because she was becoming very unbearable to be around. Also, she was not the only one grieving, we all were. I just thought she was having one of those moments and overlooked it. No, it was much deeper, and when I went to her house that Tuesday, something in my spirit said don't go back over until the day of the funeral. Something had shifted and the energy was so bad off I didn't even want to come back to her house anyway. On the flip side, I knew that if I did not go back between Tuesday and Friday, they were not going to be prepared for the funeral on Friday, so I was uneasy but obedient.

Lo and behold, exactly what I thought would happen, happened and much worse. I got ready for my grandmother's funeral at my friend's house. As I was doing my makeup and hair I got a call from my sister. Even through the phone, I could feel her energy, my friend could feel it, and we both heard it. My friend was in close proximity to me helping me get ready, plus my sister was loud. She was letting me know the funeral cars were at the house, I mean that wasn't shocking, it was maybe 10 a.m. and it's customary for the funeral family cars to arrive at the house early. The funeral wasn't until 12:30 p.m., so I explained that to my sister. She then yelled into the phone, "Okay then, because I'm probably not going to be ready on time anyway," and hung up abruptly. Me and my friend both looked at each other and she said let's just stop and pray. We did, after that, I continued to get ready and got to my sister's house around 11 ish. I sat in my car and waited for them to tell me they were ready so I could just go to the limo. As I waited, I got a call from my Mother asking where I was and I told her I was sitting in my car. She then asked me if I could do something to my niece's hair. It's 11:30 ish y'all, but I obliged, it's my niece. As soon as I started working on my niece's hair, she started making excuses for my sister and that immediately pained me. This is exactly what I used to do for my mother's shortcomings and it's very unfair for kids. Then it's like 11:45-11:50 and at that time the drivers are asking us to get in the cars and my sister is nowhere in sight. My mother decided that she was not going to be late for her Mother's funeral and said we should leave, so we got in the car.

We're ready to go and the drivers are not moving, but asking who Krystal is. I answered it's me and they put me on the phone with the funeral director, to basically say they weren't going to move until I okay the other 3 family cars to return back to the funeral home, due to set financial obligations. The other family cars were for my sister, her kids, and husband, my cousin and his 8 or 9 kids and wife and lastly my uncle and his family. My uncle, his wife, and kids drove their own car and neither my cousin nor sister showed up at the house before we left for the funeral. So we finally left and made it to the church just in the nick of time. That was one of the worst rides of my life, and not only because we were heading to bury my mother, but because my sister called and cursed out my niece and berated her for leaving for the funeral. She literally was only mad that my niece was in the funeral car with me and was threatening her. Then my mother and I simultaneously started arguing, because I told her if she laid a hand on my niece there was going to be a fight, we argued about her having no type of authoritative skills or accountability with my sister. She casually overlooks everything that is happening. Granted I will give grace, she was grieving at the moment, but this is also a pattern of hers. All I wanted to do was say goodbye to the physical part of my grandmother and then get right back out of Birmingham. I was literally holding on by a thread and wanting to explode like a volcano on the inside. You would never know though. I was very poised and took good care of everything. We get to the church and more things start to go awry. The person who was supposed to open up the service with a song is nowhere to be found. Then, my sister comes in late and loudly with one of her friends. The service is now flowing well then as the pastor begins to open up the eulogy, something happens that is reminiscent of a Tyler Perry movie or dysfunctional dramatic cinema. My sister's friend interrupts the pastor and blurts out that my sister did not get to see my grandmother's body before they closed the casket. The reverend simply said, "Ma'am, please have a seat, we will open the casket back up after service, we are going to do things in order." I lost it and just walked out. There was no way I could sit still, I was so embarrassed and all of this was so uncalled for and preventable. I mean the uncouthness, the disrespect, the plotted demise of a smooth funeral all was way too much for me to sit and control my anger any longer. I left before the Pastor could continue. I think God just lifted me out of my seat because there is no telling how the devil would have used me if I had stayed. Self-awareness is so important and no matter how much you love God, how much you have changed your life or blossomed, at the end of the day we are all humans and there's only so much any of us can take. Triggers are real and you have to know what to do in the face of them. At that point the devil could have had me screaming, fighting, and arguing right there in that funeral, reverting right back to everything I have fought so hard to evolve from. That was my tipping point, I left with a line of people behind me trying to comfort me, but honestly, none of them had the words, they were just as shocked, appalled, and angered.

That was the funeral, but let's move on to the repass. It was so awkward. I was the only one of my granny's girls there to represent, in a room full of mostly strangers. My mother had left because her daughter had loudly and angrily told her to bring her her car. Plus, there had been issues leading up to the repass that had me already annoyed with some of the people at the repass. Someone offered physical help and then mistakenly took me accepting the offered physical help of helping hands for money, versus people serving. I had to have a conversation with that person's partner so that they understood I was never asking for money. I would never try to come up financially at someone's funeral, plus I was not broke and had not been for years. It was just another irritating, possibly miscommunication, but still aggravating thing to deal with. Funerals are tough to deal with, people show either their best or worst sides while grieving and disregard everyone else around them. I just happened to be the one that took the majority of the fallout, because I was the unofficial, unplanned, and unasked-for "Leader." The deaths and funerals were just the beginning of this new healing journey I had to embark on. The deaths were not only extremely hurtful, but they unearthed a new level of exposure in me and the people around me. I was exposed to the true condition of what I would be doing now and in the future, leading. There were also new places of needed healing and growth revealed. I now had to grow at lightning speed to manage, cope, and continue with all that was happening.

7

The Aftermath

All I wanted to do was leave after the funeral. My favorite cousin was asking me to stay another week for Thanksgiving. I should have never obliged and left, but I love my cousin and I also felt I needed to be there longer for some reason. I don't know why honestly, because I really felt so out of place. I had recently come back from living overseas and may have spent a combined 4-5 months in Birmingham, before eventually moving to Atlanta. I took the first 4 months of 2021 off and then traveled professionally to other states during the last bid of the Pandemic. During that time, I was no closer to my family then, than I was before I left. I was situated among people I hadn't seen in years face to face, or I only saw in passing when obligated or just had overall been estranged from. My father and mother were still blocked and had been for the past 2 years (We didn't attempt counseling until 2-3 months before the deaths). I literally was and still only close to my favorite cousin. Her parents and her mother's side of the family are more like family than my own extended family. My father's youngest two sisters and I are very close (the one right above them and I have embarked on building a closer relationship), my grandmother of course, my nieces and nephew, and my friends. Now, my father and I relationship has grown a lot since our completion of counseling. Me and my mother's relationship is still one that is a work in progress, I'll get into that more later. The majority of my known family members live in Birmingham and yet, the above sums up who I am in contact with. My sister right under me and I had grown closer and started operating like real sisters again when I returned to the US, and then during the funerals, boom, everything changed. I think that is what bothered me the most about our situation. As I was returning, my sister was recently let back out of jail and awaiting her trial. She would call and beg me to talk to her, send me cash apps, etcetera to try to grow our relationship. She was also previously on the block list because she came at me wrong while she was in prison. I told you guys in book one that I had to eliminate/block/take a break from anything and anyone that was not serving me or keeping me from healing and I meant it. She clawed and clawed her way back into my life, just to turn around and flip right back on me out of nowhere.

After the funerals, there was more drama, no rest or grieving for the weary. My sister was calling me and leaving messages that sounded extremely dysfunctional. When me and my mother were talking, she would try speaking to me and that would end between us arguing through the call. It's like she forgot how badly she acted in front of family, friends, and strangers. Not only that, she had so much to say about me. Whatever she was feeling we could have sat down and talked about it, we were on good terms and a conversation would have been honored and accepted. Instead of talking to me, she walked around with a nasty attitude and purposely wanted to ruin the funeral. She literally was overheard saying that she wasn't getting in the family cars (This is why she was so pissed that my niece got in the car. She purposefully did not want to be in the cars) and that she was on her own on time and would get to the funeral when she felt like it. Also, she said that we were having the funeral too quickly and why was I always in control. None of these things said directly to me and all things that could have been said/asked beforehand, instead she purposely sabotaged the funeral. When we did have one conversation and I tried to hear her out, it all just sounded like she was pissed at me. I mean she made it clear when she stated what she was mad at me about, which meant she should have been mad at our mother and family friend as well since they had said the exact same thing as me at the exact same time. Yet, she only had smoke for me. The quote, "It's cool when they do it, but it's a problem when I do it," reigns very true. It was such a fickle thing that made no sense for her to act the way she did, and this is not me dismissing her feelings, because I don't like it when someone does it to me. It's just apparent that that reasoning seemed masked by something else she has yet to reveal, because again had that been the chief reason she should have been equally mad at our mother and their friend.

I was now right back slap dab in the middle of the toxic and chaotic relationship with them I had previously escaped. I had not been in this type of disorder in over two years, since I had decided to distance my-self from all of them. So, that in itself was too much. Then I had many prophecies that were spontaneous and random that painted the same picture. I was surrounded by few loved ones and needed to be aware of the jealous people and the ones that had centered themselves as my enemies somehow. I wanted nothing to do, but leave. In the meantime, I was trying to do things that would give me relief and help aid me but nothing was working. Well, for one reason, even when I tried, more things would arise, and I was constantly being put in a position to handle things. There was my sister's lawsuit against the motel that we were trying to file since we had a witness, but later as stated previously the witness backed out. Then my sister had other legal business she never handled before her death that I was trying to handle, plus deal with her estate, while also trying to get resources in place to help with the kids. I was trying to handle her things, gear up to go back to work, and find space to grieve. I tried working out. I was so fit before the funeral. If you read book 1, you already know I had lost over 115 pounds naturally. By now I had plastic surgery to eliminate the excess skin that was left behind after such a massive weight loss. I was snatched and I was constantly in the gym to maintain all I had worked hard for. I went to the gym and literally could not work out. As soon as I was trying to work out so many thoughts started pinging around in my head. I was emotionally and mentally weighed down and I could barely just walk on the treadmill. I felt weird and guilty being in public when I had just had very public deaths happen. Grief comes with so many emotions and these were only the first things that had begun to weigh on me. Then, of course, it was the holidays, so I decided to be around my family. Well, thanksgiving rolls around, and here we are "one big, happy family." Then in walks my great uncle, the one who had molested my mother, sister, and I recently found out a cousin of the family as well. Not only was he there, but he also kept telling his niece to get my attention and tell me to come see him. I could have vomited and then I no longer wanted to be around my family. Like does anyone not see how even his presence is damaging? Did anyone not understand that the bathrooms had two stalls in them and that another molestation could have easily happened again in real time? I am constantly accused of being too "deep" and "overreacting," but what I really am, is passionate and vigilant. I could see how yet another generation could experience this curse any second and just felt like I was the only one concerned and could see it. That was Thanksgiving, and after that, I finally went home.

I was finally able to decompress well, kind of, because back to work I eventually had to go. Plus, my deceased sister had a preliminary hearing that was only 2 weeks away. Things never stopped piling on. I got a small break and was able to decompress some when I took a trip to Miami in December. I was able to sit on the beach, cry, pray, and hear from God. He spoke a lot of things to me and I was fine for a while. After going back to work at the end of December, I ended up planning and going on a trip for a friend's birthday near the end of January. Then at the beginning of March, I celebrated my own birthday, which was so needed, because the week leading up to my birthday grief was trying to crash me out and I could tell. I literally just was having obsessive thoughts about my grandmother and her leaving me. I then went to DC for a speaking engagement in the middle of March and hung out with my friends. After I returned from DC, my sister was convicted of murdering her boyfriend and given a lengthy sentence. I drove home to be with the kids before I left for Germany to visit my friend. I went straight to Germany and stayed until the second week of April. While I was in Germany, I got a call from one of my imprisoned sister's friends. She was calling me, at the direction of my sister, to try to tell me something was going on with the kids. I instantly panicked and started calling back home back to back to no answer. I then finally got a cousin on the phone and she explained to me that my great uncle who again had molested several people in the family was around the kids. Fury really flashed over me and I wanted to fly home instantly. At this point, we are driving from Brussels to Amsterdam and I am crying the entire way (Bless my poor friend Dani, I thank her for enduring my drama on our trip). I finally talked to my mother and got the understanding that yes he was there (again he should be nowhere around), but nothing happened. My niece had told my sister while on the phone with her and then my sister had her friend call me. I was in a different time zone, so I missed the call, and since I do not answer calls unless they come in from WhatsApp, (My close family and friends know to call me on there if I'm traveling). I had no idea who it was that had been calling me and why until I listened to my voicemail. I immediately got upset after listening to the message and wondered how and why you would be calling me from prison. Why would she be giving your friends my number and have them call me? We hadn't spoken since the funerals and now when something is wrong per usual I am being called. That's another thing that has always been the premise of the relationship with my mother and sisters. They will literally talk crazy to me, disrespect me, or we have this big falling out but as soon as something happens, I am supposed to ride in and be the hero. On top of that, it is usually when something is way out of control that I have no previous knowledge of, but somehow I am supposed to know just what to do to fix it. In this season, all of this was really weighing on me and I just kept taking hit after hit while trying to maintain my own day-to-day life. Before traveling to Germany, my travel contract had ended and I was in the market for a new job. When I got back from Germany I started looking for jobs and going to interviews. I kept looking in Georgia and Alabama, I just felt the need to be close to home, especially near the kids and again I was reminded daily by others that the kids needed me. I ended up getting hired at a job that was a pay cut from my norm, but also a slow-paced job where I would have the opportunity to slow down a bit and try to heal. I really had not slowed down since the funerals. My life was still moving at lightning speed and although I minorly felt the implications of needing to sit down for a second, I had not made time to really explore that sentiment. Even if we don't take time to slow down and explore ourselves, God, our body, or something else will do it for us. In my case, my emotional turmoil and a new onset of depression did it for me.

8

Hello Depression

I'll never forget May 1, 2023. I had my first day of orientation at my new job. I had worked out, showered, cleaned my place, and was on my way to bed in preparation for the next day's orientation. I lotioned up and laid my head on my pillow, feet rubbing together and just about in rem sleep, then out of nowhere this thought ran across my mind, "Dang! My grandmother ain't called me to ask me about my first day of work." Suddenly, I was sitting back up and wide awake. That one thought had shattered any type of sleep, rest, or well-being I thought I had or wanted to have. Everything in me had to come to the realization that my grandmother had passed and she couldn't call me. It was like finding out she had passed all over again. Also, no one called and asked me how my first day was that day. It was like solidifying all over again to me that I have no one else. She was my everything, she never missed anything in my life and cared and covered me in the big and small things. I did not feel like I could and would ever have anyone else in my life whose bond was as deep and tight as ours. I also trusted her. We really worked through our differences in the past and she respected my boundaries. I'm telling you, we were seriously best friends, except she was my grandmother, my best friend from a different generation that I was free with. She would tell me her secrets and experiences in life and I would tell her mine. We always laughed. She would give me great advice and good sayings or her point of view on things and I listened. At that point in my life, when she died, I had no other person I felt as close to, especially elder. Most of my relationships at that moment were growing/rekindled relationships. Remember, I had just moved back to America. So, to better understand what I mean, let me give some examples. My aunt Tomica and I had just started being around each other every day and we were building our relationship. It was solid, but not as solid as it is now. Kameisha and I had rekindled our relationship, from us being distant, to hanging out and talking daily after I got a place in Atlanta and was settled enough to nurture a relationship. Really, once I returned home and settled down, I was able to nourish a lot of relationships and meet new people. But at that moment, I felt like everything I ever had on Earth was gone.

That night was the first night that my depression had deepened. I think the first trigger or time I started feeling like this was the week before my birthday. I had a few days off and was not doing much and had time to myself. I would find myself crying or just thinking about my grandmother a lot. Just thinking about how I wish I had more time with her and then soothing myself with the thought that she was no longer suffering here and that she was tired. Those are true, she even told us on the car ride from my sister's funeral that she was tired. Even though those thoughts were justifiable in a sense and true, they did not erase the pain or eradicate my feelings. That time of settlement and grief was quickly overshadowed and I was able to really perk myself back up with the excitement of my birthday and going to the Ari Lennox concert later that week. Even this time was temporary, but was longer. I cried that entire week and barely got out of bed. My orientation was virtual, so I just got up long enough to be attentive to that. The next week came and I had to go to the hospital and, of course, I was going to be together for that. I have the great ability to really get it together and function at the worst of times. I can mask well what is going on with me without even trying. It's true resilience that has helped and harmed me. I just keep going, I handle what needs to be done regardless of how I am feeling or what is going on with me and later suffer for it. I will touch on that later. I go to work for two days and then to Belize later that week. In Belize, I am around two of my favorite people in the world celebrating their birthdays. So, all is well. Nothing is bothering me, I am having fun and I am surrounded by love.

Then I get home, back to work, then my niece's 2nd birthday party, so my mind is there and I am having some therapy sessions and things are okay, I'm okay, I believe. Then the world throws me another blow in which grief and depression escalate. I talk to my mother on the phone and for weeks, months even, I have politely asked my mother to not talk to me concerning my sister who's incarcerated, for obvious reasons. Plus, I would be feeling better and doing well and then my mother would call me in total disarray, understandably considering what we all had been facing. The problem with that is I am currently in my grieving phase, but wanting to heal and move along, whereas she was still okay with remaining in the same state. The realization of that difference led me to identify that there was no way I was going to get better if we kept trying to heal together or if I continued to be her emotional support. Then in therapy, my therapist literally confirmed my thoughts even though I never told her my thoughts about what was going on. She said to me in a matter of fact way, " You and your mom can not heal together." I was discussing this with my mother and also asked her if we could not discuss my sister because honestly, our relationship and how it had dissolved was still a trigger for me, and anything concerning her outside of the kids I wanted no part of. My mother kept bringing her up because she was being sentenced and that had nothing to do with me. To make matters worse, I got a court appearance notification to appear in court on a case where my sister used my identity and got a ticket in my name. I said these things to my mother in the nicest tone I have and asked politely again for the 1 millionth time, that she not discuss my sister with me. By the way, she responded to me, you would have thought I picked up the phone and called her everything, but a child of GOD. She was spewing so much hate, negativity, and false doctrine about me that by the end of that conversation, I had to resort back to blocking her. That conversation was the straw that broke the camel's back. It had been such a hard, lengthy, taxing, and emotionally draining 6 going into 7 months. I was tired, not just physically, my soul was tired. My mind was tired, my body (I wasn't working out as effectively as I used to, but was barely eating and still gaining weight), all the way down to my pinky toe, everything was just tired.

Depression came in and hit me like a wrecking ball. I had no idea how to even sum it up to that, but the side effects that I was exhibiting all pointed to depression via my Therapist. I mean my thoughts were consuming and awful. I am not a person who overthinks regularly or has a billion and one thoughts that I can't easily subdue. This was different and the thoughts were loud, suggestive, and would not quiet down no matter how hard I tried to subdue them. Every thought was negative and pointed to either wanting to die or trying to commit suicide. I would wake up in the morning and before I could even pray, open my mouth, or even feel myself being fully awake, my mind would say, "Ugh, we woke up again." Then it would go on to, "Why were you praying? God does not hear you or care." I will be at work quiet, but my mind would be ping-ponging off the wall, thoughts would be like, "I hate this job, why am I doing this?" Or "Don't talk to these people, do not even get close to anybody just do your job and go." Driving home I would hear, "Crash your car, your grandmother is the only person who really loved you anyway." Sitting in my living room I would hear, "Jump off the balcony." These thoughts would play on a loop violently and from the time I woke up, until the time I went to sleep, if I went to sleep. I was barely eating and my prayers were not as strong or as astute. I wasn't clear about anything, everything was skeptical. I was crumbling internally. I then started praying that God would just stop waking me up. The thoughts were too much and I just suffered with it. I kept working and doing my daily activities, meanwhile, my brain was attacking me. I talked to my therapist and she told me, Krystal baby, you are depressed. I literally laughed, because me? Depressed? Looking back now, I don't know how I ever thought I wasn't depressed or didn't realize this was not even my first time going through depression. I had never even explored depression as it relates to myself. Also, I was taught growing up Black and Christian that I was not depressed and never to claim or speak that. The other thing is I think I was so used to living with so much that I never looked at it as more than being, just my life. I have only known true peace in short spans of my life, so all of these things going on were just the norm for me, but these thoughts were not. I think one of the events that opened my eyes even more and sort of justified what my therapist had said is that I went to church with a friend one Sunday, and at service I began to cry and could not stop. I mean I cried and cried, I knew it had nothing to do with the service because this pastor's sermon was not that effective to me and was very milk-based. By now my spiritual level had matured tremendously and the sermon he was giving I could have given in my sleep. I think what may have triggered me was the pastor had recently lost a friend and the friend's family was in the audience. They brought the family up and there were two kids, a girl and a boy, and the kids were looking around awkwardly and sad. I think that picture just made me think of my niece and nephew. I cried the entire service and the drive home, I stopped at the wing stop, grabbed my food, and was still crying. I pulled into my garage, so blinded by tears, I scraped the bumper of my car pulling into my garage. I went upstairs to my place and cried the entire day. It was awful. I already hate crying, it just confuses and frustrates me unless it's under the spirit of God or tears of joy. I just feel weak and like tears don't mean anything. I am still working on understanding them for my own personal well-being because I truly am pressed about it. I just got through years of being numb and now have to really explore, understand, and feel my feelings. I don't think I have ever cried like that in my life and was now more willing to hear what my therapist had to say about depression. We talked and she suggested I may need to look into taking antidepressants, specifically SSRIs (Selective serotonin re-uptake inhibitors). I listened and then got to researching. I don't take advice or suggestions about anything unless I take it to God first or/ and research it first. One of the main SSRIs that most people take is Zoloft. I researched it heavily and even remembered conversations with people who have taken it and decided against it. Instead, I wanted to try a more holistic approach which was CBD. I read that CBD does the exact same thing as SSRIs and without the side effects. I went out to the stores and talked to CBD reps and landed on one, prayed over it, and started taking it. The next thing I did was cut off all vocal conversations with everybody. I explained to those close to me what was going on and why I was not going to be answering any calls. They understood and were very respectful of my boundaries which is more than I could ever ask for and exactly the type of people I have prayed for in my life. It wasn't that they were a part of the problem, it's just that I am the type of person who doesn't like burdening others. They love me so much so whatever goes on with me bothers them and this is the same way I feel about them. Also, to many of the people around me, I am the leader, the strong one, and what I feel or how I act can and has dictated their emotions as well (Leadership is a gift and a curse). More importantly and specifically for this time, I wanted to eliminate all outside noise and voices (Guard your ears). I only listened to gospel, stayed off social media, and didn't watch television.

At that moment, I did not even realize what I was doing, but I was definitely starving the devil from any resources to attack me. I may have been depressed, but not only that, the devil also was trying to do what-ever he could to keep me in this depressed place and bondage. I would be minding my business and he would whisper things to me like, "Let's go out," "Let's get drunk," "Call one of your exes, tell them to come through," "Hit the blunt," do this, do that and so many other things that were outside of what I was no longer doing or running to. This may not actually sound like horrible things in this society, but trust me, whatever you run to outside of God to deal or cope with your problems has become your idol/savior in some way. In the past, those were things I would run to, but at this stage of my life, had I not learned anything? Yes, I have. So I had to fight those whispers tooth and nail. During this time, not only was I being exposed to the tricks of the enemy, but again I also was simultaneously maturing spiritually. These were things I had grown to not do regardless of the desire because of my commitment and growth in Christ. There are other things and my Christian journey continues, but also what good would any of those things lead me to? Yes, there's nothing wrong with a good party, but excessive partying can be a problem, financially and physically, and can contribute to loss of focus. Drinking is one thing, but getting wasted is another. The implications of addiction, possible DUI, health problems, not being sober-minded, being susceptible to harm in this world, etcetera. Calling my exes for what basically? Other than sexual sin and manipulation, plus possible pregnancy scares, more toxic behavior from either of us, and who knows what else that could lead to (all that playing back and forward is how a lot of couples wind up on the news for abuse or death). I don't love those men and the power I have over men I have dated can be used for all the wrong reasons so I stay far away from them. Marijuana again, addiction, loss of employment, a deity. Everything in life should be done in moderation, free will or not at all. We should not be running to any substance, thing, or person to deal with life's issues, that only keeps us in bondage. The devil knows this and his goal was to entice me back into everything I have fought hard to break free from. This is the cycle that too many of us get caught in. The days turn into months, months turn into years of the same battles over and over again, meanwhile, time and life continuously pass us by. I refused to be caught up in the same things I broke during my first healing journey, even if I slipped, I would get right back up and repent and turn away from it. I understand what going back to any of those things implies, which is to me a lack of growth. I define growth as simply learning from your mistakes and refusing to do them again. The perpetual cycles only rob us of energy, time, and education. Without those 3, you are literally running but getting nowhere, basically jogging in place. So I shut off all sources, and I just got alone with God. I journaled, walked, worked, took my CBD, went to church, prayed, and allowed Him to seep deep inside of me and help me out of the hole the devil was trying to get me into. Suddenly things started to get better. My thoughts started slowing down and became more positive. My mind became more clear and I was able to draw certain conclusions that made sense. I was able to pray better and stronger. I was able to start talking back to my circle, started working out again, and got back to being social. It was working and when gathered with 2 of my aunts in prayer one day, a breakthrough happened and full deliverance took place. I never felt the same after that prayer and I have not felt the same since.

Depression is real and it affects more people than we know. I get how hard it is to admit or even understand what depression looks like. Especially in those of us whose lives have been filled with trauma. So, sadness seems normal. Also, a lot of us grew up in households where if you said you were depressed, we were met with aggression or anger and told, "YOU'RE NOT DEPRESSED!" or "YOU HAVE NOTHING TO BE DEPRESSED ABOUT!" Grief and everything else I wrote about previously led to my depression in that season, but there are countless things that can trigger it. Also, nothing at all can be going wrong or seemingly bad in your life and it hits you. So, someone saying that you are not can easily detour from looking into what's going on or finding the right tools to fight the early onset of depression from becoming worse. That we perish from a lack of knowledge is not just some random quote, but is actually from a Bible verse (Hosea 4:6). That verse was centered around the people of that time rejecting the knowledge of God and His law. Today we can apply that same verse in every place where knowledge is readily available, but we fail to consume it or apply it. This was a deep and hard time for me and I now see God still had a purpose for it. One way I will be able to break the generational curses in my family and community is by applying the things I have or am learning and spreading awareness.

I won't pretend to have all the answers for grief or depression, I am just sharing my experiences and showing the things I was able to do to heal and maintain a healthy lifestyle while hurting deeply. Also to note, I only had to take CBD for 1 month before I became more regulated in my thoughts and actions. I do take them here and there if I'm particularly going through a hard time or a very rough day. Everyone is different and some people have to take prescribed meds, CBD or medical marijuana, and some other things. I want to be clear that we are all different and I think you should do the work to find out what you need personally. Grief is one of those things that live with us throughout our lives, we literally lost a part of our DNA and genetics. We were intertwined with these people from a chemistry aspect all the way to a physical aspect. Then there are people you may not have any DNA ties to but have a solid bond with and their passing can affect us on a deeper level as well. We can't choose to turn those feelings off, but we do have the power to manage ourselves in a healthy manner. Sometimes I laugh at things my grandmother or sister did or said. Sometimes I cry at the thought of them. I never know how or when I will express my feelings about them and that's okay. I do know that I will not be consumed by grief, depression, or anything else and I also know that neither my Grandmother nor sister would want that for me. We can't die with them, we have to keep living until God says it's our turn. Refusing to get up and fight for your life, happiness, and well-being is also a form of death. This is what I would call the "Walking Dead," and I know the devil delights in every second of this type of existence. I don't want him to have any delight in my life and even beyond that I was not sent to this Earth in this shell to live like that.

9

⬥

Generational curse breaker + Generational blessings

What's a generational curse? I read this on Christanity.com and think it sums it up perfectly. It reads, "A generational curse is believed to be passed down from one generation to another due to rebellion against God. If your family line is marked by divorce, incest, poverty, anger, or other ungodly patterns, you're likely under a generational curse." The Bible says that these curses are tied to choices. Deuteronomy 30:19 says we can either choose life and blessing or death and cursing. Our families have the greatest influence on our development, including the development of our patterns of sin. Some people even assert that family or generational curses are passed down along generational lines. This belief comes from Old Testament passages which say that "God punishes the children and their children for the sins of the fathers to the third and fourth generation" (Exodus 34:7). Whether or not, families inherit spiritual curses. It is obvious that patterns of sin are passed down through families. Everyone sins; but just as culture, ethnicity, and gender steer our patterns of sin in particular directions, so do our families.

In the last chapter, I briefly spoke on how learning and applying the knowledge I have obtained is breaking generational curses in my family and community. In this chapter, I want to expound on that sentiment and also give very eye-opening examples of generational curses I have seen at work in my life and family. It's not just the toxic or bad people in our families we have to get free of, but also the bad traditions. Not all traditions are bad, but there are some that have to be called out and extinguished. I will use the example of my great-uncle molesting my mother, sister, and others. That could have possibly been prevented from happening to my sister if he was exposed/punished and not let around other kids to do the same. The uncorrected behavior continued to wreak havoc for at least two generations (that I am fully aware of), it kept passing down, so at this point it can be seen as a curse. The toxic interdependence of my mother, grandmother, and great-grandmother stopped this from being a revelation because they kept it among them and my mother was persecuted in the same way my sister was. Toxic interdependence is now a tradition and if you go against the herd mindset or behavior you are disowned for it. They frame it that you're breaking away as a lack of loyalty. Loyalty is important in all kinds of relationships, but there are times when you have to be wise, regardless of loyalty. Loyalty should not allow bad to live and thrive. Family secrets like this cripple the entire family, as well as, the mindset of those that refuse to believe the victims. I chose not to stay silent any longer when it happened to my sister a second time. This is what breaking a curse looks like. Learning, growing, and applying what you have learned. Some people carry a mantra of, this is just how things are or this is how it always has been and they never try to correct or change the narrative. Then there are those traditional phrases like, "teeth and tongue fall out, but they still have to coexist," or "That's still your momma, brother, sister, uncle, etc." There are people more dedicated to this ideal of family than they are to the healing of individuals and the evolving of the current family concept. There are thousands if not millions of people suffering from the wounds of their families and they cannot heal while being gaslit or having their feelings downplayed.

Another curse I seek to abolish in my immediate family is the incarceration and the incarceration effect. One of the things that bothered me the most during the funerals is, in my reflection time, I just kept seeing how parallel my nieces and nephew's lives are to our lives at their age and so many instances, I saw and heard us from them. This was how me and my sisters lived growing up. Their set up is even like ours now. They now have an incarcerated parent and a form of a parent abandoning them. Although my sister is deceased, kids usually internalize any instance of a parent leaving them as abandonment, not to mention the absentee fathers. It's like seeing my mother and my father all over again. All I saw when looking at the kids, was us. They are not even my kids, although I love them like they are, but I don't want what we experienced for them. I can't say they will internalize or interpret their situation the way we did, but I know there's a possibility because history repeats itself and again it can be passed down through genes, socialization, and reality. There have already been some situations where the things they are experiencing have affected their lives or they have expressed it emotionally (I won't be discussing those things). I will say the difference between them and us is they have an aunt who is fighting for not only them but the next generation as a whole. They are informed about the predators in the world and our family. They are taught to speak out in a respectful manner and are assured they won't be penalized for it. They even have more family members willing to help out with them, than what we did. My mother is in some ways better with them than she was with us. They don't have a 100% better life, but they are having a slightly improved experience, especially where it matters. If they choose to listen, incarceration will not be a part of their story. This is a generational blessing on their end.

I know my sister's incarceration story is not only a curse from my father, but also from my mother. My sister has known nothing, but toxic relationships since she began dating. To be honest, we all have experienced toxic relationships, but my sister's relationships have always resembled my mother's. One reason I think her relationships were like this is because we grew up watching and behaving in the same way my mother did with her men. We saw my mother date countless men, she was young and had no real concept of a good relationship herself and tried to go about dating in her own way. She just wanted to be loved and so she ran into men who abused her, misused her, cheated on her, and also abused us in ways. I was never the one to stick with a man who would put his hands on me or even call me out my name. A man I was dating at one time called me the B word once, and that was the last time we ever talked. My mother and sister were the exact opposite, both had lengthy relationships with men with whom they had multiple instances of verbal and/or physical abuse. The toxic self-worthlessness of staying in something so dysfunctional is what led my sister to prison. Fighting for her life in a toxic relationship that she could have easily left, caused her to have to defend herself to the point of taking her boyfriend's life. I can't blame my mother for the murder, but her choosing to stay in those situations definitely had an influence on my sister. Also, my sister refused to listen to any sound wisdom from anyone. Children rarely do what you say, they do what they see you do. I have behaved like what I saw in relationships and had to develop an entirely new way of doing things. I learn from my own mistakes and other people's mistakes and make those learned lessons law in my life, trying to never repeat the same things twice. I often think about what was applied and not applied throughout my lineage to shape who I am and what I have experienced today with my family.

Another generational blessing I have seen over the last two years is the gifts of God. Speaking in tongues, prophesying, hearing from God, and being a prayer warrior are something I have learned a lot about in my family after stumbling across them in my own life. I grew up in church with my maternal Grandmother. She loved God and taught me everything she knew about Him. She either did not have or did not express her spiritual gifts to me. I grew up and started going to church on my own and one night the gift of speaking in tongues came upon me. In this past year, prophecy has been spilling out of me. I never had experienced something like this before. Now I have been right about a lot of things and can discern well when I use discernment, but this is different. It wasn't until I started talking to my aunts and them actually hearing and seeing me operate in my gifts (which are completely spontaneous, I never know when or why, the holy spirit just springs up inside of me and takes over) that I was told that this is something that my paternal grandmother and great grandmother both possessed as well as several other family members. I know these gifts are blessings from God and my aunt teaching me how to use them and understand them are a generational blessing. These types of gifts can be terrifying when you first experience them, especially if you have never been accustomed to them. I did see people prophesying and speaking in tongues eventually after I left my grandmother's church, but I had never experienced it in myself. My youngest sister had some of these gifts, she often spoke of Christ and heard Him, but some things scared her or she thought she was crazy. I wish she knew what I know now to be able to accept the gifts and steward them well. These are a few of the blessings and curses I've noticed firsthand.

Being the generational curse breaker is a unique experience of its own. I think everyone can be one, anyone who sees the wrongs, and instead of going along with them, speaks out and refuses to go along with what's happening. I came into this world with a lot to say and was often chastised behind it. The things I had to say were because I did not understand. How can we say we love people and then as soon as they leave out the door we have all these negative things to say? How can you say you care for people, but instead of offering sound advice without judgment, you talk about them? How are we family, but everything feels or is made out to be a competition? I was confused as a little girl when I saw things and I always asked questions. I will never understand being envious or jealous of your loved ones. I will never understand being around people acting fake. I either like you or I don't; there is no in-between. My mind was made up a long time ago on how I would operate and, I have held to my own set of standards constantly. It is hard being a generational curse breaker. It will come with more scars in the beginning and maybe, no promises or trophies in the end. Being the first of anything comes with a lot of pushback. Examples of people like Martin Luther King, Malcolm X, Sojourner Truth, Ida B Wells, and Barack Obama are all people who either came first or rejected the norm. They have scars to prove it and some lost their lives to their beliefs of change. I am in no way, shape, or form comparing myself to these great people, but I am painting the picture that when you choose to march to a different beat you're going to be met with conflict. My conflict may never be as big as theirs, but it has been life-changing. I have been talked about by family members, disowned, questioned at certain family gatherings, looked at funny, told I was against the family and the list goes on. These things are actually small compared to what the people I listed faced, but I know in some of our lives it is just as significant and emotional. The generational curse breaker have to really be okay in the face of being set apart. Just think of Jesus, He came to save the world and look how He was treated. The very people He came to save hated Him. The very people He called family did not believe in Him. The very people He tried to teach rejected Him. He cried also, and he was isolated at times. As an agent of change, this is just a part of your story unless others get on board with you. If not, then it's just you and for me, that's okay. God actually did not leave me on my own. He has given me a community of like-minded individuals who have the same goals as me, which is to eliminate as many toxins, negativities, and dysfunctions in our generation as we can so that the next generation can be better. This is the goal on a family level and community level. Complacency is an enemy of change and growth and it is an enemy I am committed to fighting.

Each generation has similar instances as the previous generation. The Bible says that there is nothing new under the sun (Ecclesiastes 1:9), so we know that we pass along things from generation to generation. Again, the goal for me and mine is to pass down as much life as possible and eliminate those things that lead to death. What we do in this generation will surely produce fruit in the next whether that be good or bad. The goal is better, not perfect. Perfection is not achievable. We all will sin and fall short of the glory of God (Romans 3:23).

10

Reinforcing Boundaries

In my first book, I talked about setting boundaries. In this book, we are going to take a deeper dive and talk about reinforcing boundaries. Boundaries! Set boundaries and stick to them! I have heard this before and I am sure you have too. I will even say I thought that I was good at setting boundaries but realized I was with everyone, except my family. It is one thing to not let people get over on you here and there or certain people, it is another thing to stand on your boundaries daily with everybody. I remember reading an Instagram post that said, "Train your mind to be stronger than your feelings and your boundaries to be stronger than your empathy," the poster ended the caption with my same sentiments, "Whew!" This resonated with me so much, because this is something I have had to do over the years, and never had the words to sum it up as eloquently and accurately as they did here. What's a boundary? A boundary is a line that marks the limits of an area; a dividing line. In other words, a place that cannot be crossed. When dealing with family, living in the same households, depending on each other, and thinking family is your everything, we loosen or drop the boundaries necessary for us to be healthy. Let's be clear, I come from a strong family. My Mother, Father, Grandmother, and more are very tough people and always told me to never let anyone play with me or disrespect me, yet, when it came to them that notion was non-existent. We have to operate with everyone the same in order to achieve the highest level of respect and peace. A Harvard Business Review states, "Boundaries are limits we identify for ourselves, and apply through action or communication. We define what we need to feel secure and healthy..." This is easier said than done especially when you are a part of a toxic or dysfunctional relationship. As a part of this current healing journey, I have had to create and reinforce a lot of my boundaries.

Let's walk through some of these instances and see where the root of disregard for myself and my boundaries came from and how I reset my boundaries.

Example 1, as I talked to others about my deceased sister, they told me things she would say, I listened and one thing that became very clear to me was that she saw me incorrectly. I was not viewed as her sister, but more so as her mother/savior. This led her to have a lot of resentment towards me and I feel like everything I did try to tell or teach either of my sisters was constantly met with rejection or rebellion. Instead of them seeing me as a big sister looking out for a little sister, they were taking my advice as me trying to be their parent. Her resentment towards me was inappropriate and misdirected because I am not her parent. There were no boundaries set for our roles in each other's lives and the ones that should have been established from birth were blurred because of our upbringing.

Example 2, my mother, sisters, and I have had a toxic interdependent relationship for many years. The best way I can describe it is that it is like a feeling of needing to be separated, but every time you try to leave or get away something always draws you back in. There is also this constant cycle of dependency and strife in the midst. I saw this with me when I decided to move out on my own after our childhood chaos. I was repeatedly berated for trying to better my life, which meant breaking away from the tribe. I also saw this when I tried taking my sister in while in high school and she acted a fool, but she was so pissed off when I gave her up. Then, one sister got pregnant so I got an apartment with her, we sat down and made rules and agreements with each other. Then my other sister and mother moved in with us and all the rules and boundaries we established within our home went south and our living situation ended badly. I told y'all in book one about another time I tried to protect one of my sisters and what she said to me after being arrested (see chapter 4 in Read My Story, Hear God's Glory). Another example of the toxic interdependence is with me leaving and going overseas to work, there were comments about me leaving like I was leaving them in particular. I was even accused of trying to run from our problems (really their problems) by them. This is so unfounded because I applied for that position strictly to elevate my career and out of exploration. I am glad I left because it gave me some distance and growth to see where I needed to set boundaries with them and stand firm in my own identity. It also helped me to not feel like I had to be the hero. I have said several times that I was always being called when something goes wrong and honestly at one point a part of me took pride in being there for them. I was tethered to trying to change them and be there for them in every way when in all actuality the only person who could do that was GOD. I can help or support here and there, but I can't be and do everything. That only led to burnout and my own resentment.

Example 3, another toxic/boundaryless thing that affected us is this unspoken rule of loyalty between the four of us that I feel like I shattered was having my own mind and not agreeing with everything they said or did. We have very different perspectives and ways of living and doing things. I feel like I was always judged for not being like them. There have been verbal attacks and a lot of secrets to easily prove this point. I am always left in the dark because of their fear of me telling them the truth or giving them sound advice. This doesn't just apply only to our foursome, but also throughout my family and many other families. Boundaries could have stopped, changed, or never allowed any of those earlier examples to occur, but boundaries are tools that healthy people have or people are educated on altogether. This is not something I was taught or saw often within my family. I also now realize that people who were trying to establish boundaries were somehow being talked about and made out to be anti-family. I was young then, but now I fully understand and set boundaries clearly and do not let anyone cross them. As the saying goes, "You either stand for something or you fall for anything," and that is what boundaries are to me, your STANCE.

Family can be very cultish and is the first place I had to free myself from. Some people's entire identity is tied to their family. It is extremely hard to turn away from people you love and everything you know, to do and be better in your own life. From the time we are born we are taught family is everything and family is all we have. I am here to say a healthy family with established and respected boundaries can be amazing, but family will never be all we have. That statement eliminates the other healthy relationships outside of family we can create. Some people don't ever experience a healthy biological family, so should they not go out and experience love and health elsewhere? It also eliminates the fact that if we have nothing else in this world to cling to, we have God. Boundaries can help with all of this. Those 2 years I blocked my mother, sisters, and father were the most peaceful years of my life. Yes, I had some things going on here and there, but never a daily, weekly, or monthly fiasco. I told you earlier that my youngest sister and I were estranged before she died and my other sister had clawed her way back into my life and was consistent so we had a great relationship, up until the funerals. I also talked about me and my parents going to counseling months before my sister's death. This was a boundary I set initially between my parents and me before they could be in contact with me. I value myself in a way no one else can, but God. I cannot and will not let anyone on God's green Earth disrespect or treat me in any old kind of way. I know who I am and what I bring into other people's lives and I won't be short-changed in return. The boundary of counseling is the first place my mother dropped the ball. After 2 no-shows of our counseling session. I blocked her again. I only unblocked her when my sister died. It was necessary, but after the funerals, I should have blocked her again. I know this sounds harsh, but stick with me, you will understand by the end. I should have blocked her again because the issues we had before the funerals had not been resolved. The funerals just overshadowed the issues during that time. As soon as something did not go my mother's way, like I stated that day we had that big argument, every problem and thing I had been trying to talk to her about in counseling and resolve came tumbling out of her mouth in pure vitriol. You cannot heal from a wound that keeps getting reopened and this is exactly what was happening here. After everything I had done to protect her and our family, planned her mother and daughter's funeral, did her hair so she could look presentable, etc., and let's not even talk about everything she has done or allowed during our childhood. I was yet again back at square one with her. We would have never had to have another dramatic falling out again like this, had I blocked her again and demanded counseling again as her only contact with me. Here we go again and this time is the worst because she is my only contact with the kids. Now, I am going down this road of what to do with kids? This blow-up happened right before my nephew's 13th birthday. It hurts me so bad to have not shown up for him, but I could not be around my mother. You can't keep kicking people and then expect them to show up for you, like my grandmother used to say, "Hell even a dog gets tired."

My mother at that point did not know boundaries or even have respect for me or anyone else. She has been enabled her entire life, by other people allowing her to do things to them. She will show her entire behind to them and then things would just fall back into place without any type of real resolution. Never any accountability being had or consequences for her behavior. I am not one of those people. I have not asked her to go above or beyond with me but to show me pure human decency. Your kids are not the dumping ground that you get to disrespect or whatever else and expect them to want to be around you. I am not built like that and this is something she has come to understand. She stayed blocked for months after that, we only talked about the kids when needed. My auntie would pick them up for me and drop them back off. I did not attend her birthday party and I can only talk with her if the conversation is respectful. When you grow and heal, it's so hard to be around people who haven't. That old saying that describes a person having a better chance of pulling you down than you pulling them up is very true. I had to reset the tone and lay the land between me and my parents (My father and I have been on one accord since our completion of therapy). There is no room for any scribbling outside the lines in our relationships because they have been strained for years. That means reinforcing anything that seems like it's creeping up on violation. It is now March 28, 2024, and she has been okay since Oct/Nov. I cannot control her, I am only in control of me and what I allow. That is why that Instagram post screamed so loudly at me. Your feelings will have you doing and accepting the unusual. God specifically told us in Proverbs 4:23, "Above all else, guard your heart, for everything you do flows from it." In order to be a good steward of my heart, I cannot allow anyone to come in and stomp all over it. Our feelings and love for a person can cause us to get away from the standards/boundaries we've set and we start retracting back to our old habits which leads us back to square one. The Bible tells us to take captive every thought (2 Corinthians 10:5), we cannot let our thoughts and feelings control our actions, especially those that do not line up with the ways of God. He does teach us love and forgiveness, but He never told us to accept abuse and to stay in unwise situations. Peace is worth fighting for and demanding, and boundaries help establish harmony. Being at odds with anyone is not a good feeling, but there can only be reconciliation if both parties are willing to change, especially the party that causes the most harm.

11

Reconciliation

I'm not going to lie, the word alone kind of trigger me. In order to be reconciled, there has to be a break at some point. So what was it? How deep was it? Usually, it's not deep at all and then there are other times that the damage is so severe that people choose to never deal with each other ever again. I get this because honestly, I have not had the desire to reconcile with anyone from my past, except one person. Forgiveness? Yes, that's different, it's a commandment, and in order to move on from a situation, forgiveness has to be had. I have had to pray to forgive so many people and I am sure people have to pray to forgive me as well. The heart is fragile and can only endure so much. One thing that forgiveness and reconciliation have in common is that both become easier when there is an apology and accountability taken. The willingness to own your actions and in some instances even be willing to right your wrongs is a true testament of a person who is sorry. In my opinion, to really resolve the situation that caused the break, it's your job to go out of your way to never do anything similar. Doing so again is just another slap in the face to the person who was offended. This is kind of why I am not really big on reconciliation. People can change, but they rarely do. I have mostly been dealing with the same situations with the same people in my life and I am sure this is why I have no space to give effort to rekindling relationships with outliers. Besides, we always say, "People are seasonal and some people are only in your life for a little while," so why is there such a big uproar when someone decides they never want to be involved with certain people again? This is exactly the crossroads I found myself at when dealing with reconciliation. I have had many relationships over the course of my 17 years as an adult. Relationships with people from my neighborhood, people from high school and college, people from church, people from different programs, different states, and literally all over the world. Out of all the relationships that had to end , only one relationship I would reconcile. I was the person that broke that relationship. I have apologized, taken full responsibility, and left the door of opportunity to rekindle open, it is now entirely up to them to want to do so. If they never do, I understand and I cannot be mad at them about it either. We are cordial now. This is the only person that I can truly say, "Me and this person may have been lifers or had a longer season of friendship (an old high school friend that I stopped being friends with at age 19 or 20). If I stop dealing with someone I had a close relationship with, there is a well-thought-out reason why. I know who I am, what I bring to any relationship, and what I will and will not tolerate. I am also reasonable and understanding when approached with situations. We are all humans and make mistakes, so some things can be talked out and moved passed. The hurdle is the person who broke the bond, being big enough to come out and say they were wrong in the first place. Then there are other things that are so bad that there is nothing left in that situation, but to part ways, forgive, and move on. Some relationships were never that deep in the first place, so moving in different directions is okay and understood. Then there are relationships that leave a lasting imprint on your life that you never forget and you learn from, whether good or bad. These may sting a little bit and take a little longer to process and/or let go of. Then there are relationships that should have never happened in the first place like: trauma bonds, codependency, and abusive relationships.

I have had a lot of relationships, so I know a lot about relationships and one of the most difficult relationships I have had is the one with my mother. Especially on this road of reconciliation. I am telling you now, that this chapter may continue in books to come, but let's get into what is privy to this book. Just like anyone else in my life, I have had no urge to reconcile with my mother. In all honesty, I don't even see her like a mother. Like yes, I know she is my mother, she birthed me, but we are two very different people and she did not raise me. My grandmother did and is who I refer to when asked about my mother figure, my mom is just, who carried me in her womb. We are majorly disconnected and so different. It's like I can say the sky is blue, she will say it's purple, or I can say the grass is green and she will say it's brown. It has been a rough 35 years between us. It all started from my birth, she says all the time my grandmother took me from her. That is probably where the beginning of detachment started with us, I never bonded with her appropriately, because I was with my grandmother and she had 2 more kids right after, back to back. We were in and out of each other's lives for years. I stayed with my grandmother as I got older for years by choice. I never liked my mother's friends or the people she exposed us to, I had a lot of discernment even then. I was wise at a young age and had a mouth and she would be pissed at me for running it. She was a teen raising us and not by any means having things together. I give her grace in that. I could not imagine having three kids by 23. I'm 35 and can't imagine having 3 kids now, but 23 is so young. Most 23-year-olds don't even know themselves, haven't seen the world, still making mistakes and some just graduating from college. So, yes, she made hella mistakes, I mean probably the same ones that most teen parents do. She also never listened to wisdom, I think now at 54, she's just now starting to listen to some things. Her adult life has been rough and honestly, a lot of it has been from a series of bad choices. This is something she speaks of frequently. I would be lying if I said that she did not warn us about her mistakes. She did, but again most kids don't do what they hear, they mostly follow what they see, either consciously or unconsciously. I have even fallen into some of the same mistakes she has done in my past. Letting anger lead me, fighting first and asking questions last, being involved in some illegal activities, and so on. The only difference between me and her is some lessons I refused to learn twice and I pursued God in my younger age, so my transformation started younger. I am a lot more spiritually in-depth than she was at my age. I am literally teaching her about bad theology and reading the Bible in full for yourself. We have positive similarities too. We both have smiles that can light up a room, even with her gap, she has a beautiful smile. We're both strong, independent women. We're both social butterflies, we both know how to be hospitable and know how to turn a house into a home. We are similar, but nowhere near the same. I assume it's God or grief that has me trying to work things out between us. I have rarely attempted to work anything out with anyone and definitely not for this long in my life. Who cares if she is my mother, if she constantly hurts me? Being a mother does not give a person unlimited grace in someone else's life. People's parents have died and they never reconciled, my sister died and we never reconciled and I, just like many other people have said, have no regrets in that area. Intentionality does not matter when it comes to matters of the heart. If you hurt someone, you hurt them, no matter how big or small you think it is. Between this book and the last, I can list 100+ different ways in which my mother has hurt me. Possibly, even in ways she doesn't even realize, because people like me who do not walk around with their emotions on display are often overlooked for having no emotions at all or almost seen as not human and not needing help/comfort. My father and mother both even admitted in therapy that they never paid much attention to my needs because they felt like I was ok and did not need them as much. I felt this a lot during the funerals, not just from her, but in general. I don't think you have to be a wailing widow for your pain to be seen or felt, I think you just have to be around people who are aware and care about you.

Through therapy and letting go I have been able to forgive my mother of everything in our past, but it is so hard to get to the present and future with her because she has not forgiven herself and taken full accountability for her wrongdoings. She also often reverts right back to nasty habits between us. I told y'all earlier that you have to fight to not go back to what you are used to doing, choose something different. She is just now grasping that, and her lack of doing so has been one of the main sources of our contention. This is my mother and everything about our relationship feels unnatural. Honestly, on my end, I have given up. I mourned my family a long time ago and everything I participate in now I do for the sake of my nieces and nephew. They deserve a healthy, loving family. They deserve holidays spent together, peace, and joy. I'm willing to stick to trying to build a good relationship with my mother, for the LAST time, for them. Even though it's for them, I still have to protect myself and my feelings as well. So, we can only do this with the right boundaries in place and with her being dedicated to change. I am not going to lie, it's awkward for both of us. Things haven't exactly flowed together in harmony. We are both figuring things out. She sometimes attends counseling and I do as well, but not together which is something I think we will eventually have to do together again. It's a lot of mixed emotions. I personally don't even know what I would want from her honestly at this point in my life outside of consistency and respect. It's like stumbling in the dark because I never know when she's going to jump ship and stop doing what she's supposed to do or simply revert back to how she would behave previously. We have a hard time communicating because she is always distracted or does not return calls back, she forgets to tell me important things or we bump heads during the conversation, etc. I am asking for equal sharing of commuting to see each other. She never came to see me during those 4 years I lived in Abu Dhabi, now I'm only 2 hours away, so there's really no excuse for her not to come see me. These are things I find extremely difficult to navigate on my end. I talked to her today and asked her what she finds difficult to navigate on her end in regard to reconciling with me. She said she feels like she always fails to live up to my expectations. She says that she is scared when we talk that we are going to argue if she says things the wrong way and she has to find out what she can and cannot say to me. She says she misses when we did have a bond, spent holidays together, and being a real part of my life. This reconciliation thing is a heavy burden for both of us. It comes with a lot of tears and headaches. A lot of arguments, a lot of feeling lost, and a lot of strain. If you know me then, you'll know that I avoid all of the above at all costs, so this is not something I will choose to do often or maybe ever again. We have made some small progress, I see some very small changes in her. She goes to counseling and it seems to be working. She definitely listens more, I do have to walk her off the ledge of offense from time to time because she doesn't know me enough to know when I'm joking. I have to reiterate some things often, to make her understand why I am saying things and to let her know my boundaries. Our relationship broke so long ago that I think she often forgets that I am grown. This is a hurdle we have to overcome because you have to respect your adult children differently and I think she understands that the more we converse. Even though I am not the one who broke our bond, there are still things I have to do differently in order to have peace in the reconciliation as well. This is hard for the offended! I have started repeating Proverbs 19:11b "It is to one's glory to overlook an offense." I know I am further along in my healing journey than her, so I have to first recognize where she is and respect where she is as she continues to grow. In the aspect of holding her accountable in situations that arise, I have had to simplify things and explain rather than just go off. I have to be the bigger person in conversation sometimes and get the conversation back on track, by taking down my voice, taking a breath, and/or restructuring what I am saying. Sometimes we have to hang up, every conversation can't be had in real-time. Sometimes, we need time in between the conversations to approach the issues differently or have a cool-off period. I know it sounds like a lot and it is. I don't know if it's worth it yet and may not know for many years. I know she feels different because I am her child and she's the parent. I think, for me, I will probably feel accomplished once I am able to feel the love I say I have for my parents. I don't just want to say I love them, I want to feel it. It's a long road, but as long as we stay steady I am willing to try. Will I ever be able to trust her to the point I can share my private life with her? Will I ever feel secure with running to her in the time of need/help? Will she ever see me correctly? I don't know. I can only focus on day-by-day interactions and that's all God even asks of us in Matthew 6:34 where He says, "So don't worry about tomorrow, for tomorrow will bring its own worries. Today's trouble is enough for today." Like I said earlier in this chapter, this will be a continuing subject, I just hope that at some point the subject has progressed more in the future and is more positive.

***

I completed this chapter on April 2, 2024. On the morning of April 11, 2024, I had a conversation with my mother, which started off well and ended in flames. There was no redirection working, no boundaries respected, and no accountability taken about a situation that happened 17 years ago. This is after having an in-depth heart-to-heart conversation in December at breakfast about our previous behaviors and responses to each other and what lines shouldn't be crossed. On this day, she crossed every boundary we set in that conversation in December and went even further. I am updating this chapter versus rewriting this entire chapter or book because I want to be transparent and accurate as I write these final lines. To reconcile with someone, there have to be two willing parties working together, respecting each other's boundaries with a dedication to grow the relationship. This has not been our story (Two willing, but only one respecting and actually working for evolution) after four dedicated years of trying (2 years blocked 2020-2022 and then trying since August 2022, starting with therapy, she missed 2 consecutive sessions and then we parted ways. My sister died the following October, we reconnected and all that you've read up until now.......) and years of previous, forgiving and overlooking offenses, I am done. I have no desire to ever try again and I am okay with us parting this earth estranged. If it be God's will, then so be it, but I will follow his decrees and demands despite my feelings, otherwise the relationship is severed. There are some people you can reconcile with and then there are some you can't. Everyone won't understand this because of what society and the world tells us we should behave, act like, etc. I don't follow this world's values and trends. I will be praying to forgive her for this recent incident and I will set myself free from this emotional and mental abuse, bondage, and burden. I'll never reach my full potential or the next level being bound by this situation between us. I used to be able to keep going, despite our issues, but now after so many years of it, I don't function like I used to after our major blow-ups. I'm different now, my mind is different and I don't live and breathe toxicity, so I'm affected like a person that has never been in these situations. We throw the word toxic around in such a light manner, but anything toxic to you is poisonous/lethal and leads to death. Maybe not a physical death, but a mental and emotional one and that is just as bad and can also lead to a physical death, depending on how you cope with it. So, the things that go on between us are more catastrophic for me in my current place of life and healing. I have to save myself or I will be back in the same spaces I fought to get out of mentally and emotionally or die in those areas altogether. This upset has tried to pull me right back to where I described I was last May. High-functioning depression, which can lead to stagnation and setbacks, but no, I'm not going. I love my nieces and nephew so much. I even have had to choose my own mental health and well-being over our relationship to stay out of her presence. I have been wounded for years, but I'm not a little kid anymore and I choose me. I've decided and the final decision will always be me.

12

Identity

Who do you think you are? Who do people say you are? What composes an identity? What does identity have to do with this book?

These are questions that came to mind as I stared at the title of this chapter. Our identity is what shapes everything in our lives and the lack of identity is where so many people get into trouble. There are some parts of our identity that no matter what everyone sees, there will be a certain set of standards, customs, specifications, and/or norms that come with it. For example, I am a human female. That is obvious in any setting and there are certain things that are attributed to that. Having a softer voice, more breast tissue, curvier body shape, being born with a vagina versus a penis, menses, etcetera. Then there is the part of our identity that comes from our culture, lifestyle, family, environment, and what we come into agreement with. Our identity is influenced from birth and we mostly hold true to the things we come into agreement with. I myself have had a strong awareness and definition of my identity from a very young age or I will say my perceived identity. Good, bad, or ugly, I have held true to what I thought or think is me. Where we live, how we are raised, what we hear, what we believe, and what we see all impact our identities. Identity is important to this book and to me because I have had to allow my identity to be transformed and shaped anew over the past 2 years. It has been a constant change and at times the changes have left me very confused. I really want to express it here, because I know countless others who are experiencing this or will experience this identity shift. As my grandmother would say, "Live long enough," I will add, live long enough and actually grow during your life and you will surely go through an identity transformation. Everyone will be different in how they transform and how they handle their transformations. I think I have done well in this season of transformation, but not so much maybe in others. I can say this because in other seasons, I allowed a cycle to ensue, I wasn't completely open to or accepting of the process or I wasn't even aware of the transformation. I do have a feeling that this season and the transformation I am going through right now will set me up for everything in this next phase of my life, if not for evermore.

My new identity has only been born from me choosing to surrender who I think I am, for who God has called me to be and submit to His directions. As stated earlier, from birth our identity is being shaped by our experiences and agreements. I read this book, called The Four Agreements by Don Miguel Ruiz, he did such an excellent job of describing this. If someone calls you dumb and you believe it or you come in agreement with it, then now that's a part of your identity. You are always going to associate yourself with something somebody else said about you if you believe it and agree with it, even if it was said 30 years ago. His book tells us we have to come out of agreement with everything everyone else has said about us, especially the negative things.

One thing I have even said in my previous book about myself is, I am a fighter. At one point, that has been a leading characteristic in my life. I was known for physically fighting in Middle and High school. I was then known for verbally fighting in the comments on social media over injustice, politics, culture wars, and so many other things. I am still a fighter, but I now allow God to fight my battles or guide me on when to say/do something or when not to at all. There is a different framework and context of fighting surrounding the way I operate now (New Identity). I have been on the verge of biting my tongue in half while trying to keep my mouth closed in places the Holy Spirit was telling me to hush. Baby, it takes restraint to back down when you know what you are capable of. A good example of this is last year as I was relaunching my first book, I wanted to take it a step further and hired a production company to film a podcast for me and record me audibly so I could release an audio version of my book. I researched and prayed and after going to meet with the owners of the company I felt secure enough to work on the project with them. I even sent them over the requirements of the audio recording per audible standards before making a final decision. They assured me over and over via email it would not be a problem. Well, after months of recording and filming, there were problems. Firstly, not one deadline that was set was met. I was offered an excuse for the deadlines and kept abreast and I did oblige new deadlines. I finally received the edited work and there were many errors. When asked for editing in the beginning I was met with no problem. Then after having to comment multiple times about the same thing, because again there were errors, the texts started becoming very passive-aggressive and I was being gas-lit about my concerns. Imagine paying in full for services and being told that any issues would be handled. Then after bringing up issues and concerns over the errors you find, you are then told that the company has done all they could do and they don't want to work with you anymore. They gaslight you and say that they don't have the capacity to serve you because you are requiring too much. I only required the things we agreed on and then they still never delivered a recording eligible enough to pass Audible Standards (I had to seek out and pay an outside source to get my final audios done). I'll never forget receiving that final text. I was at work, I wanted to just clock out and meet them in their office with a baseball bat (to put it very lightly). I was fighting mad as the old people would say. It is really something to put your trust, time, and energy into something and have people play in your face or treat you like you're the problem. I remember I was about to respond, and the Holy Spirit said, "Wait." The message I was about to send was going to be so lethal that nothing I could have done physically would even amount to it. This is something else I have had to work on and reshape in my life. I have been known for being a person who can, "read," "clap back," or "curse" someone out real good. I'm very quick-witted and know how to pick up on people's insecurities fast. This characteristic of mine can be used to motivate or destroy, depending on how I use it. At this point in my life, I am dedicated to always trying to do and be my best (One of the four agreements from Ruiz's book). In this situation, the next day after venting and having so much anger and venom circulating inside of me, I finally calmed down with the help of my aunts and friends. I then remembered who I was. I am a business owner with a contract in place, I can simply sue. At that thought, I had to laugh at myself. Operating in my old ways would have me in jail or regretting my words after being convicted by the Holy Spirit. My new identity says, "Why operate in the old when I have accepted the new?" I came out of agreement with handling things the way I would have. I actually think before I respond, I can still speak up for myself while sticking to the facts and points and without resulting to cruel insults. God has these things handled, vengeance is His and everyone will get their just due. Even as I type and assess this, knowing it is the right thing, I will honestly say I still struggle to come to terms with this. I want immediate action, I want God to send thundering bolts of lightning to fry people who've harmed me unprovoked and so carelessly. Unfortunately, this is not the way He handles things and no matter what I'm feeling, I still have to revert back to trusting Him, even if it seems like others are not receiving their just do. His ways have proven to be better, so I keep believing in Him and pray for my unbelief when I don't.

Owning my identity and following God's will also means coming out of agreement with things that even people you love and people who care for you say about you. I have had to do this for many years. People will mislabel, misquote, or misidentify you in a heartbeat. I have evolved at quantum leaps in this season in my life. So, things people may know to be true about me today can easily be untrue the next day. Also, people have tried to press how they feel on me or how they think I should feel or handle different situations. Again, these are well-meaning folks, but even with them, I have to interject and correct what does not align with me, my spirit, or my identity. I am quick to tell people "I hear you." And that's what you feel/think but I don't agree with that or that's not how I feel/think. It is something I have done on numerous occasions, you have to really stand boldly daily in your identity or this world/people around you will shape everything about you. We were all meant to be unique, God made us special, so we don't all think alike, feel alike, or process alike. So, why would I allow anyone to tell me who I am and how I should feel? I have no problem with anyone voicing their opinion, but I have the right to not agree with it. Telling the people you love, "no," seems impossible at times, but it's necessary for what you are specifically called to do. Whatever decisions I make are well thought out and are processed through me and God. I do have counsel who I know are wise and make good decisions in their own lives and I run things by them from time to time, but emotions can easily sway us. When we care about people, we tend to feel like the way we would do things would be best in their lives, but that's not necessarily true. We do not know their assignment, promises, or position. We also have to really take time and distinguish between what's right versus what's perceived due to our emotions. Love will have you thinking and acting crazy about stuff, but we have to be mindful at all times. Our loved ones' decisions need to come from their own thoughts and filters through Christ, they have to own their own identity the same way we have to own ours. I had to get to this point, the few times in my past I allowed what someone else was saying to me to be my truth or listened to their advice, all ended badly. Do I blame them? No, because I did make the final decision, but influence is real, especially when coming from those you love. Those instances taught me a great lesson. If you are going to receive advice or opinions, meditate/pray over it before you decide, and let God lead you to your final decision.

Another topic I want to broach while speaking on identity is the lack of identity and the consequences/pitfalls that come with it. I have watched so many videos on TikTok and YouTube from people talking about how they started serving other Gods, doing witchcraft, or just making bad decisions after bad decisions because they did not know who they were or the truth about God. It is so easy to think things are not that deep when you don't know the truth. Like, for example, think about getting your palm read, reading your horoscope, or calling a psychic, all seem so harmless. They aren't harmless though, especially when there can be spirits and/or idolatry formed in those spaces. The videos I watched of all of those people, had bad outcomes and returned to Christ later. Most in some form or another were suffering from identity crises or lack of identities that led them to seek out something, anything to soothe their misunderstandings. Life will really test you and what you believe. I am not here to blame or shame anyone, I know what it is to be off the right path. I know what it is to be searching for anything to fill your voids. I thank God for His grace and mercy and my praying ancestors that I am constantly being led back to my roots and connection with Him. Even now on a deeper level with God, with a greater understanding of Him, I am still being challenged by different things. When you know who you are and whose you are, you can't be persuaded otherwise even in the darkest moments or times. I have spent so much time reading and learning the Bible over these last couple of years because there is so much knowledge of who we are in His word. There is so much of what God says we should stay away from in His word. There is a wealth of guidelines, wisdom, and practical sense in the Bible. We say life has no manual and the Bible debunks that as a lie. People who don't know who they are don't just fall into alternate religions, but identity crises also lead people to gangs, drugs, prison, etc. Ignorance is a tool the devil uses so blatantly against us. This is why from young, praying over your kids, having them repeat affirmations, and instilling in them who they are is so important. They don't have to agree with everything and they do at a certain age get to decide what's best for them, but those positive attributes will aid them in seasons where they are questioning things. God's preferred ways are always proven to us somehow. It's not always immediate, fun, or makes sense in the beginning, but somehow the picture being painted becomes clear. I'm telling you, the things God has spoken to me or I have read in His word are not even things I probably would have chosen for myself, yet, He is the creator. Would you argue with Steve Jobs about Apple products? He created it and can tell you every intricate detail about it and how it works. So, arguing with him about an apple product would be futile. In the same way, God is the creator of us. Even with that being said, I know the difficulty of trying to sit back and trust God, yet it still feels like you need to do more, say more, or just rely on your own understanding. In my experience, trying to fight against His words or urging has only confused me more or caused me to overthink. Deciding to rely on Him has been another new challenge in my life because again I am a strong, confident, and very smart woman who has done and accomplished a lot without this level of reliance on Him. Now with my better understanding and growth, I know that true wisdom is surrendering to Him, letting Him be strong in the places I am weak, and allowing Him to show me the areas that need addressing. Identity, like healing, is something we must be flexible with and carefully manage at every turn of our lives. Relying on God and our set morals and values is the only way I have seen fit to truly help guide us in times of great testing. With that being said, don't be afraid to fail because we don't always get it right. I do encourage you to not give up and keep faith in God (Even if it's just a mustard seed because honestly, that is sometimes all the faith I have had during all these storms). Let your identity be who you truly are, but inspired and influenced by God and the positive attributes of this world. He never said don't be you, but He does want us to be influenced and led by Him.

13

Showing support

This chapter is sort of a bonus chapter, inspired by the many people that I hear say I don't know how to show up for other people and the people that would say to me that they felt like they weren't doing enough for me during my time of mourning.

Let me start off by saying, "There is no one way to be there for other people and everything doesn't have to be overdone." A simple text to show you are thinking of someone is support. A hug, smile, or just listening to someone speak is a show of support. Support looks different in every season and levels of bonds in relationships. I would not expect someone I barely talk to or don't have a tight bond with to, all of a sudden, start showering me with love, support, or compassion. That is kind of unrealistic, although it can happen, but I wouldn't expect it and I don't think others should expect that either. During my time of grief, I had people show up for me in various ways. I had family, friends, and coworkers show up, cook, and serve for my sisters and grandmother's repast. I had people send money for the repast, family that took over the repast. I had one friend literally take an Uber to my sister's repast, helped set up and serve, and worked remotely during the repast. Also, I had a friend who literally cooked me breakfast and was by my side every day. I stayed at her house during that time and even went and served at both funerals. I had a friend drive from Atlanta to Birmingham just for a few hours to spend time with me and bring me clothes because I was running out of the few clothes I packed since one weekend turned into an entire month's visit. I had friends send me flowers and cards. I had a friend send me affirmation bracelets. I had a friend give me a handwritten thoughtful card and then I had friends that just came and sat with me, listened to me talk, let me cry, and encouraged me. I had people send me inboxes and DMs on all my different socials. All of these meant something and all of this stood out in my mind. Not one thing was too small, showing your support doesn't have to be a grand gesture and anyone expecting a grand gesture every time to show support is surely insufferable.

I did speak out during my time of grief once about people not showing up for others during these times of need and my speaking that one time was the only time I mentioned it. I spoke because there were people that I felt were close to me who should have, at least said, "Sorry for your loss." There were people that had been in close proximity to me and weren't saying anything at all or if they did say something it wasn't in support of my mourning, it was about some other non-important stuff. People were inviting me to concerts and asking irrelevant things that were clearly a show of not being able to read the room properly and at the agitation of that I made a post. It was never to condemn or make the people who were doing any of the things I spoke of previously feel like they weren't doing enough. To be honest, I was met with so much love, affection, and support that I had no time to dwell on those who weren't supportive. I placed my focus on the people who were around and I still do. Those other relationships put roles in perspective about who those people are and where we stand in each other's lives. I'm actually grateful for the revelations because honestly, I never want to be going over and above for someone who wouldn't do the same or at least have enough awareness to see that I'm hurting. I am a firm believer in reciprocity and the only time I make exceptions is when I know the person does not have the capacity to give their 100%. In relationships of any kind, in some seasons you may have to be there for, uplift, and empower one person more than they are able to do in return in that season and that is okay. If that person has been giving equal or more shares of support in other seasons, then why not? We don't always have it all, at all times. God created us to help each other, there are so many scriptures about this and it is true. I have had to help others in their low seasons and others have had to help me.

With this being said, I do want to remind us of two things: Boundaries (Again! In this context) and Acceptance.

Boundaries are needed in every facet of your life and with every relationship of your life. If you go around giving, giving, and giving, there are some people who will take, take, and take. You have to know when to say, NO. People will take advantage of your kindness and make you out to be the bad guy when you stop doing it for them. I used to have a friend I supported through college and well into her 20s. I always gave back to people in college because I struggled so badly in college and I knew how hard it was getting through it without proper support. I felt sorry for her, she was having so many issues, financially and mentally. I started out doing this without boundaries. Later, when I started trying to set boundaries with her on my time and finances, I became the bad guy and I became one of the people who was doing her wrong. Yet, I did nothing but support her for years. Now her anger is definitely misplaced, but I won't place all of the blame on her. I failed to place the appropriate boundaries with her from the start. Boundaries can be as simple as this, don't do anything that can threaten your own mental health or that can cause you to struggle in places in the long run. To elaborate more I simply say this, "Assess yourself before you give to others." If you are on the verge of a mental breakdown/depression or something similar, then no, you do not have the capacity to sit around someone grieving, hurting, etc. So what you can do in support is a text message, card, or DM. If that is all you have to give at that moment, that is okay, that is the 100% you can give at that moment and you still are giving something. You don't have to be forced into these societal narratives that basically tell you that you have to put yourself and your mental health in jeopardy to be a good friend. Good deeds have to come from a good place or they are just performative. Forcing yourself to do something you don't naturally want to do or don't actually have the capacity to do is only sabotaging yourself. You are going to pay for it in the long run. I free people all the time and ask them, "Hey, do you have the capacity for what I am about to say?" Or I simply shut down and my only form of communication with people is letting them know I am alive. I don't want to pour things that are too heavy onto others or lash out on them during my own suffering, that's why therapists are handy and God tells us to cast our burdens on Him. My close friends and family also respect this and don't do anything more than text me or if they do call it's to pray and that's it. This is a mutual boundary set between us. I shut down communication and they don't try to force communication. I am self-aware to know that I am a processor and sometimes I need space. I have communicated this with them and they have accepted it. I am also self-aware enough to know when I do need help and I will say, "Hey, let's pray or y'all pray for me I am going to listen until I can join in verbally myself." Are there times when I have set aside my own personal sufferings and given 110% to people? Yes. This still should not be the norm or a requirement in any healthy relationship. If I decide to offer up more, it is because I know that person is going through something I was called to help with. I love them, and they would do the same for me. Also, 9 times out of 10 whatever I have going on at the moment is not that deep and whatever they have going on is not going to harm me further. Money boundaries are another thing. Should we help out others here and there, yes, but my belief is only if you have it to give and you won't need it back. There is no guarantee that the person you loaned or gave money to will give you your money back. We all have the same 24 hours to make something shake in our lives. If you are able to walk, talk, lift, and bend, you are able to have some type of income. No one is responsible for providing a lifestyle for you, not even your parents once you are grown unless they just want to. I have seen people who are disabled have work-from-home jobs, work at Walmart, etc. I had a billion jobs before I graduated college and since graduating in the times I was in between assignments. I have driven Lyft and other odd jobs to keep my income versus depleting my savings. People will use you if they can. Just because you make more money than others does not mean you are obligated to give them your money. The economy is horrible and people are barely making ends meet, but that still does not mean that every month, 2 weeks, etcetera, they can always borrow money from you. If it is led by you and you don't mind, then no problem. But if you are feeling used, then just stop. You have zero obligations to do it. Also, when you stop, see how that person reacts to you and that will tell you everything you need to know about them and y'all relationship. I had a cousin ask me for $20. I had already given him money before and this time decided to say no and wished him the best and ended the conversation with I love him. He never responded. That told me everything I needed to know. Any other time he tells me how much he loves me; this time, it was blank. That love was contingent on what I did for him and that's not the kind of love I want. Am I mad at him? No, but I definitely understand what our relationship is and isn't. Also, people will try to count your pockets and don't understand what responsibilities you face. No, I don't have kids, but I do plan for my retirement, so I put money in my IRA, I stay in a stellar neighborhood, so my rent is not cheap, I want to buy a house so I have a savings for that, I am single woman without any parental support so I have to have "just in case savings," and I only know one person that I could financially depend on if I needed to, but would not even want to do that. So, I make sure I cover myself. I invest in stocks and also in myself. Everything I have done from writing and publishing my books, recording the podcasts, recording the audiobook, photoshoots for the covers, meet and greet supplies, the classes I was taking when I was back in school, etc., are all fully funded by me. So, no I can't always just throw money at people, because they assume I have some endless fountain of funds. People falling on hard times is very real as well and being generous in that season, I can do. But if they decide to live above their means and don't have an understanding of sacrificing things that aren't essential, then again no one else is responsible for funding them.

One other area I feel compelled to talk about is the acceptance of support. People who are used to doing things on their own, usually have a very hard time accepting support. I, myself and so many women around me, especially black women, seem to have a hard time accepting help. I know for me, the times I did ask for help, especially in college I was met with aggression or a do-it-yourself attitude. From then on I have done things myself. I come across other women who have the very same experience or they just never had anyone to do for them, so they became hyper-independent. Also, when you ask others for help, some people act like you are dependent on them, versus just needing a little help at that moment, or they try to throw their support back in your face. Asking for help should not be this difficult, but if you have been traumatized before in this area you are going to be less likely to ask for help. I do think being independent to a degree is okay, but when it gets so bad that we won't let the people we love and trust help us or we suffer in silence, then we are only hurting ourselves. Accepting support is still something I am learning to do to this day. My method of gauging whether to be comfortable with asking for help from someone is testing the people around me in my time of need and then getting a good gauge of who is truly willing to help. Even that is scary because again you have to go through the trial and error of who is worthy and who is not. Good discernment helps, but even with the best discernment, people flip, so you truly never know. I myself have been working through being vulnerable and overcoming offense in this season, so believe me when I say this can feel like the worst thing to have to do in your life. We should never have to feel like this, but life's traumas will keep you in a paralyzed state. I was for years, and I have gotten better about accepting help/love, but I am still trying to evolve in these areas. Even just coming to grips with this is what I have to do and need to do has been a struggle. Who wants to put themselves in a position to be hurt again? I have been battling myself mentally and spiritually about this very thing. I am currently reading a book called, "Bait of Satan," by John Bevere and he speaks so heavily about the traps of offense. I am struggling just reading it because I know it is nourishing, but allowing people in is a major struggle of mine. Letting go of offense is an even bigger struggle, but I would rather be set free than be ensnared by the enemy. This is a different healing journey and it's coming up right on the end of me thinking I have had a breakthrough in my grief. So in all, actuality in life, we never stop being challenged or having places that need work. Do your best, my friends, that's all I or anyone else can ask of you, and keep praying. A lot of things we need to work on or overcome can only be done through the changing and healing power of God. In those instances, our only job is to surrender the issues to Him and be obedient to His guidance in that area.

Let's recap and end this chapter with the things I suggest you ask yourself and be aware of while being supportive:

- Before you start going all out for anybody, check on you. Are you okay? Is this going to further diminish your mental or financial health?

- Do what you can within the scope that you can. If a card or text is the best you can do, then that's okay. If you can or want to do more, then do it. Grand gestures or gestures that require a lot more are appreciated, but neither should be compared.

- Do everything from your heart, if you don't feel led or know you don't have the capacity to do it, then don't. Anybody who truly loves and cares about your well-being will respect you. I will say, to be fair, communicate these boundaries so the other person is aware and not left confused. Everyone, if you truly care about that person, is due at least some form of communication.

- If you are on the receiving end, allow people to do what they will. If they judge you after, then that's on them, don't internalize that. It will only make you feel like you are the problem or make you paranoid about others. That's who they are and does not reflect you. But also remember, not everyone is like them.

- Accepting help doesn't mean you are indebted to that person. Should you be willing to be there for them, yes, but you don't have to stay in a place where you are disrespected or mistreated just because that person did a thing for you. Some people will do things just to guilt you later into keeping them around under the guise of you having to be loyal to them.

14

In conclusion...

This entire book has been written in my POV with the sole purpose of trying to enlighten and give direction from the things I have learned. As you can clearly see throughout the book, I am still learning, growing, and getting better every day. I felt led to write this book, just like my first book to convey a personal experience that some can't fathom, but to give voice to those who have experienced similar or worse. Sometimes talking to those close to us doesn't cut it, because they can only speak from a place of care versus experience. Some books are written way over people's general understanding or they are just overly complicated. Everyone ain't got time to decode a mystery when they are going through heavy stuff and need to see someone with a similar problem, process, and plan. Everyone doesn't adhere to 12-step programs or 9 guides to do ABC, blah, blah. Some people learn through stories versus instructions. I am just a simplified voice that wants to aid you in your own journeys. I don't have all the answers but what I do have is my experiences and I am very dedicated to studying my life. Living life is one thing, but studying life is another. If my personal reflections keep helping others, I will certainly keep writing books. This is my contribution to this world, this is the legacy I will be leaving behind. I hope and pray that all who read whatever I put out see my true intentions behind every typed word and that is to again, help and aid others in their own healing journeys.

Be encouraged and of good faith, because as you can see, we are all facing many challenges daily. Keep focusing on and reworking the things you can control and the things you can't control, don't try to. Find a way to get at peace with it, whether that's giving it to God (for us prayers), removing yourself from the spaces or people, or coming up with new plans at every turn of events. Lastly, and what I would consider most important, keep up your mental health and wellness. I work out, pray, talk to my therapist, go to the chiropractor, go to the spa, stretch, eat well, go to social outings, keep my appearance up, travel, do new things, I mean any and everything to keep my mental health and body well. If none of what you are trying helps, then talk to a professional, there are several medicinal and holistic aids as well. I would just suggest praying and doing your own research before taking leaps in these areas.

I can't wait to hear you guys' triumphant stories, we are all on this rollercoaster ride, labeled life together. Don't hesitate to reach out to me via IG or tiktok: krys.hughes. In the words of my therapist.....

TAKE GREAT CARE OF YOURSELF.